# Michael Pandya's Indian Microwave Cookery

*To Mohit,*
*my youngest and dearest son –*
*'baby' of his generation in the family and loved by all.*

# Michael Pandya's Indian Microwave Cookery

PRION

Published in 1998 in Great Britain by
Prion Books Limited,
32-34 Gordon House Road,
London NW5 1LP

A catalogue record for this book is available
from the British Library.

ISBN 1-85375-255-X


Printed and bound in Great Britain
by Creative Print and Design, Wales

## ACKNOWLEDGEMENTS

The encouragement and cooperation extended to me by Chris Davies and Paul West enabled me to plunge headlong into this pioneering work and wade through the rather uncharted waters. These two are friends who are always happy whenever my next book comes together. Thanks fellas – much appreciated. My bank manager wasn't too disappointed either!

Thanks to my friends Mathew and Jean for their patient hearing of my denouement of the subject matter, and for their constructive criticisms and suggestions for the betterment of this work.

My long-standing friends Beni, Dinesh and Amar, who are something of connoisseurs of Indian food, took time off from their busy schedules to discuss this book with me in some detail. Thanks boys. They are fully au fait and do understand that (notwithstanding these many years and my earlier books) I get very excited every time a book of mine hits the shops. On the eve of publication, I invariably go all goosey, like a schoolgirl who has been kissed for the first time!

All kudos goes to a young couple – Manoj, my son and Allison, my legal daughter (daughter-in-law) – for their valiant effort in getting together many of the appliances, accessories and ingredients required in connection with the writing of this book. There were others – too numerous to mention by name – who made a valuable contribution towards the preparation of the manuscript for the publisher. Thanks guys and gals.

*Michael Pandya*

# Contents

A LIST OF EQUIVALENT AMERICAN NAMES FOR INGREDIENTS USED
THROUGHOUT THE BOOK:

| BRITISH | AMERICAN |
|---|---|
| aubergine | eggplant |
| coriander | cilantro |
| cornflour | cornstarch |
| courgette | zucchini |
| double cream | heavy cream |
| pepper | capsicum |
| prawns | shrimp |
| rocket | arugula |
| spring onions | scallions |
| stock | bouillon |
| sultanas | golden raisins |
| tomato purée | tomato paste |
| wholemeal flour | wholewheat flour |

# Introduction

I am delighted to be able to place in your hands another 'first' on Indian cookery from the Michael Pandya kitchen – this time a book on the whole range of Indian foods cooked in the microwave. In the dying years of the twentieth century, the microwave is going to take off as *the* cooking appliance for Indian cuisine and will surely become the common medium of cooking soon after the turn of the century.

In order to become a successful microwave cook, you need to become familiar with the working of your cooker, just like you would do with any other new appliance in your home. The instruction book that accompanies your machine will give you the essential information. What you have to remember, though, is that your microwave is neither a robot nor an ogre. You are still in the driving seat as the cook and your microwave will do what you want it to do.

Microwaving is a 'moist' method of cooking – essentially steaming. Steam is produced by the liquid contained in the food being cooked. The trapped, moist heat of the microwave creates succulent foods, with a medley of colours and flavours. Steaming, braising and stewing are the main techniques of Indian cooking, and microwaves excel in all of these.

The use of fat (ghee or oil) for cooking has virtually been eliminated in microwave cooking and stirring is almost redundant. In terms of elbow-grease therefore, the microwave is a considerable improvement over its conventional rival. Microwaves penetrate the food up to 4cm/1.5 inches and cook to that depth at the same time, whereas in conventional cooking, the food is first heated outside, then the heat slowly permeates towards the centre.

Vegetables and whole lentils retain their shape when cooked in a microwave and do not lose their flavour or fragrance. Basmati rice comes out like smiling oblong pearls. To cap it all, it takes less than half the time to cook in a microwave than by conventional methods and it is often difficult to distinguish between the food cooked in a microwave and that cooked conventionally.

The microwave oven is one of the safest kitchen appliances around. It does not become hot, so you are unlikely to get scalded. It is also heavy enough not to tip over, like a hot saucepan. Fears about safety arise because of the unusual nature of its operation and the misunderstanding about the non-ionizing radiation emitted by the microwaves.

There are two types of radiation: ionizing and non-ionizing. The first type is harmful but the latter does not damage human cells. The radiation emitted by the microwave is of the non-ionizing variety and thus poses no threat to humans. The manufacturers additionally ensure that all microwaves stay within the oven cavity by carrying out a number of checks on all microwave oven doors.

Nevertheless, the microwave is not a miracle worker; it has its limitations. For instance, it does not brown food or boil eggs – at least not without separate contraptions – and does not deep-fry at all. So, once you get rid of the false expectations and unfounded fears regarding your microwave oven, try to develop a natural feel for it and learn to use it for what it can do. There is a wonderful delicious world of microwave cookery out there to be enjoyed.

In the microwave, energy is created at a single source and waves bounce around the inside of the cooker. This sometimes leaves cool or hot spots in your microwave, which leads to uneven cooking. This is no different to conventional cookers and you will soon get to know these. In order to ensure even cooking in your microwave, the food should be arranged towards the outside of the cooking dish, thicker parts to the outside and thinner parts pointing inwards. Try to ensure that all pieces of food are of the same size or density. Larger or denser items of food should be cooked on a trivet so that the microwaves can bounce from the floor to the base of the cooking vessel.

Resting or standing, after the food is cooked, evens out the temperature. The meats relax and become more tender and moist. Given that there is a difference between the outer and inner temperatures of food cooked in the microwave, resting of the food is almost imperative.

A lot of noise is made in certain quarters about covering the food. The simple guide in this respect is: if you would cover it in conventional cooking, do so in the microwave. Covering helps retain the moisture which would otherwise be driven out of the food. Cover the cooking bowl or jug with a plate, or invert a plate over another one – that is usually sufficient and can also provide warm plates on which to serve food.

As for the cookware, remember the microwaves are deflected by metal and therefore utensils made of metal, containing metal, or even with metallic decoration must not be used in microwave cooking or there will be arcing and the magnetron of your cooker, and/or the walls of the cooker itself, are liable to get damaged. Usually Pyrex, toughened glass or ceramic pottery are safe for use in the microwave.

The basic requirement of food is that it should taste good. That is easily achieved, but you can't cook in a microwave oven strictly by the clock. Much will depend upon the size and power of your cooker, the texture and size of the food, its moisture content, room temperature and the degree of 'doneness' you require in a dish.

For that reason, the details given in the recipes within the book (eg ingredients, their measures, cooking times) are approximate and offer no more than a general guide. The frequently used phrase 'or until' in the recipes is another helpful tip. You will need to make further adjustments to make the dish suit your exact preference. Except for delicate, fatty or sugary dishes – which attract the high density of microwaves and require great care – there is leeway in all respects. It is always wise to undercook a dish so that, if need be, you can cook it a little more. But an overcooked dish cannot be uncooked afterwards!

People have long moaned that Indian food, scrumptious though it is, takes a long time to cook through the conventional medium, and that it is not always light on the stomach. The connoisseurs of Indian cooking, with their sharp and discriminating palates, therefore demand exacting standards in food.

The conventional image of preparing Indian food is now going to be shattered. The meals produced in the microwave will be fast, light on the stomach, healthy and flavoursome. Let us all witness the new revolution in the cooking of Indian food take shape right in front of our eyes!

Bon appetit.

London
1998
*Michael Pandya*

# General and Technical Information

## THE MICROWAVE OVEN

Microwaves are short-length, high-frequency electromagnetic waves, quite akin to radio waves. They are generated inside the cooker by means of a magnetron and travel to the oven cavity through a wave conduit.

The microwaves cause molecules within the sugar, fat and moisture in the food to jiggle against each other over 2,000,000,000 times per second. This friction produces internal heat, which turns moisture into steam, and this in turn cooks the food.

Microwaves bounce around the oven cavity in circular patterns while the food cooks. This makes the heat distribution rather uneven and creates what are known as 'hot spots' (areas in the oven which receive more microwaves and therefore heat, and where food may actually burn) and 'cold spots' (areas receiving fewer microwaves and therefore less heat, and where food cooks slowly). You can ensure even distribution of energy by using a microwave oven equipped with a rotating turntable and by stirring or rearranging food while it cooks.

There is a bewildering variety of microwave ovens available, many with fancy features and gadgetry. The fancy models may look flashy and impressive but they are expensive and can be unreliable. It is best therefore to stick to standard models which are of real value in the kitchen. Consideration of the following factors will help you choose the oven that is right for you:

**Size**  The size or measurement tells you the interior capacity of the cooker. Microwave cookers can be divided broadly into three categories: small, large and medium. The small cookers have a capacity of 0.5-0.6 cubic foot and look compact. However, they are not powerful enough, cannot accommodate the larger dishes required for many recipes, and do not normally come equipped with a rotating turntable.

Large cookers have a capacity of 1.5 cubic feet or more. They are expensive and bulky; they also distribute microwaves unevenly, thereby leading to the dreaded 'hot' and 'cold' spots. Medium-sized ovens have a capacity of 1.0-1.4 cubic feet. This size tends to be the most versatile and popular, and suits everyday home cooking. Such ovens have enough power (650-700 watts) and are usually equipped with a carousel. Their performance is admirably adequate for a family of 4-6 people.

**Power**  Microwave power output is not standardized; it is expressed in wattage. The power level tells you the amount of microwave energy it can generate. The higher the wattage the faster the food cooks in the oven.

The power rating of microwave cookers is periodically reassessed. Newer models are slightly more powerful. For most dishes, though, a power rating of 700-800 watts will provide a satisfactory combination of speed and results. All dishes in this book have been cooked in a microwave oven rated 700-750 watts.

**Controls**  The assorted power levels (described differently by the various manufacturers) on your microwave cooker give control and flexibility of cooking times. Leaving aside the razzle-dazzle gadgets of fancy microwave ovens, what you essentially need are settings for High, Medium and Low power levels and an automatic timer/programmer.

**High (full):** has a power input of 90-100 per cent. It is used for the majority of cooking – meat, vegetables, pasta, bread and rice – and for fast reheating.

**Medium (half):** has a power input of 60-80 per cent. This setting is used for selected casseroles, delicate foods, and for reheating leftover foods and some breads.

**Low (defrost):** (i) has a power input of 40-50 per cent and is used for slow cooking of selected dishes such as rice or eggs; (ii) with a power input of 30-35 per cent, is used mainly for defrosting tender cuts of meat and more delicate items.

**Automatic timer/programmer:** (i) a timer may be mechanical, digital or touch-type and is measured in minutes and seconds. When the pre-set time is reached, the power is automatically turned off and a buzzer/beeper sounds. (ii) if you have a programme on your cooker, it enables you to pre-set the cooking of food at different power settings without further manual adjustment.

## FACTORS AFFECTING MICROWAVE COOKING

There are various factors which have a pronounced impact on microwave cooking and the cooking times of food.

**Shape**  The shape of food is particularly important in microwave cooking. Whilst the thick areas of food cook slowly, the thinner ones cook quickly. For faster cooking, point the thicker parts of the food outwards on the cooking dish and thinner ones towards the centre. In microwave ovens, round and ring shapes cook more evenly than oval or square shapes. Energy tends to concentrate on corners of the food. You may therefore shield the corners (eg, the bony end of chicken legs) with a suitable foil, to save them from overcooking and burning.

**Size** Pieces of food that are small and uniform in size cook quickly and evenly. Given that microwaves penetrate roughly 4cm/1.5 inches into the food, your best bet for fast and even cooking would be to ensure the food conforms to that size.

**Density** Density of food does affect cooking times in the microwave oven. The denser the food, the longer it will take to cook. Porous foods will cook, defrost and reheat faster than dense pieces of meat or vegetables.

**Composition** Fats and sugar-based items cook faster in the microwave than water-based foods; this is because the former absorb the microwave energy faster than other components. Evenly distributed fat tenderizes and helps cook food evenly. Foods with a high moisture content, such as meats and vegetables, take longer to cook than others.

**Temperature** The cooking times for food given in the recipes will be affected by two factors: temperature of food and room temperature. The temperature of the food at the time of cooking will affect the cooking times; the colder the food, the longer it will take to cook. Room temperatures vary considerably during the year and between countries. You must adjust the cooking times accordingly. Frozen foods must be defrosted first, unless you are advised to the contrary.

**Quantity** Small amounts of food will take less time to cook than larger amounts, under any method of cooking. What is of particular note in microwave cooking is that if the amount of food is doubled, the cooking time will increase by about half as much again, but not double.

**Meat and bones** Bones conduct heat in food, therefore, for even cooking, remove the bones wherever possible. If practicable, roll the meat, tying it with string into a neat shape. Boneless cuts of meat, being dense, cook less rapidly but more evenly.

If, however, meat has to be cooked on the bone, remember that the meat nearest the bone will cook faster. Shield this area of meat, unless it is being cooked in liquid.

**Sensitive foods** Foods like cheese, eggs and cream attract microwave energy. They easily overcook, so bury them during cooking in less vulnerable foods such as a sauce, gravy or vegetables, or use lower power levels for cooking them.

## ADVANTAGES OF MICROWAVE COOKING

The microwave oven, still regarded by some as the exclusive preserve of the privileged few, is set to become the common medium of cooking Indian food. The advantages of microwave cooking over the conventional medium are many. Here are some of them.

**Sitting space** There is a wide range of microwave models to choose from, to suit individual needs and pockets. Whichever model you choose, it will take little space. It is essential to allow the moisture to escape from the microwave oven during cooking. Cookers fitted with vents at the top should not be sited beneath a cupboard or shelf; those with vents at the back should not be placed against a wall. Some models have special filters to circulate air through the oven. Nevertheless, the microwave is the ideal mode of modern cooking even for the smallest kitchen!

**Speed** Microwaves require short cooking times; on average, it takes about half the conventional cooking time, sometimes even less. Variations in cooking times take place owing to the starting temperature of the food, its density, shape and the quantity being cooked. But speed offers flexibility to the cook in planning a meal.

**Efficiency** The energy in the microwave cooker is directed straight to the food, so there is no heat loss into the kitchen itself, or in heating the dishes before penetrating the food. Thus microwave ovens are regarded about four times as heat-efficient as conventional cookers.

**Economy** Short cooking times in the microwave save energy and money. Installation charges are negligible, especially on table-top and portable models, the kind used by most people. All you need is a 13-ampere socket, and it costs only pennies per hour to run at full power. Even when you switch off the cooker, the food continues to cook by means of the residual conducted heat.

**Versatility** In addition to defrosting and reheating, a microwave oven can boil, poach, bake, steam and roast; in some instances, it can also achieve a grilled effect. As well as producing perfect meals, your microwave will also cope with those niggly chores in food preparation – roasting nuts and spices, melting ghee or butter and reheating liquids – in super-quick time, thereby adding a new dimension to your repertoire, unmatched by conventional cookery.

**Defrosting and reheating** Food can be defrosted and cooked in the microwave oven in one simple operation, and at a fraction of the time it would take in a conventional cooker. Food can also be reheated when required, even after hours of cooking. There is no trace of it having been cooked earlier, and no loss of flavour, texture or quality. Easy reheating makes microwave ovens indispensable for families where members require meals at different times.

**Healthy cooking** Microwave cooking is very healthy because it retains all the valuable nutrients in food. The golden rules of healthy eating – consuming less salt, less fat and less sugar – are easy to follow in microwave cooking. This method requires little fat, oil or liquid and so preserves the flavour and texture, especially of soft foods like fish, and the original colours, particularly of green vegetables. Microwaved meat is juicy and tender. Low-fat fish and chicken cook to perfection in the microwave, as do fresh vegetables and foods such as grains and pasta. Fresh fruits can be stewed or poached in their own juices with little added sugar. Steaming, the best way to retain the natural goodness of foods, is very successful in the microwave. Also, as food cooks fast, there is little time for valuable nutrients to be lost.

**Cooking odours**  A microwave cooker creates minimal cooking odours thanks to the quick cooking times and because the food is confined in the cooker cavity. As a result, the microwave oven is perfect for an open-plan kitchen.

**Convenient**  Microwaving is a convenient mode of cooking and does not need to be confined to the kitchen. It can be used instead of a heated food trolley, and can be transported anywhere in the house: dining room, drawing room, study/library. It is impossible to achieve that with a conventional cooker. The controls are so easy even a child can operate a microwave oven. In fact, it is a good idea to encourage the children to use it from an early age; they will learn cooking and will become experts by the time they grow up.

**Cool and clean**  When cooking in a microwave oven, most dishes stay cool while the food cooks. There is no condensation with a microwave cooker. The kitchen will therefore stay pleasantly cool even if you have been cooking in the microwave for long periods. As microwave cooking is moist, you will not have difficulty cleaning the dishes, thereby reducing washing-up time. It is incredibly easy to clean the oven itself. You only need to wipe the walls and the surface with a soapy cloth, and you have a sparklingly clean cooker!

## COOKWARE

There is a wide range of microwave-compatible cookware available today. It is not a bad idea to look around and see what is available for microwave cooking. Some cookware is very innovative and even cheap, but things change fast and containers can quickly become outdated.

The size and shape of the cookware are important for quick and even cooking, especially if the shape of the container conforms to the size/shape of the food. The container should be deep enough to avoid spillage when the food bubbles up, and large enough to hold food spread out evenly in one layer. If you choose containers suitable to cook in and serve from, immediately your washing-up is halved!

Let us now have a look at what is on offer.

**Plastic**  Dishwasher-proof plastic containers may be used, but not to cook food with a high sugar or fat content as the cooking of these takes the temperature to very high levels. Boiling/roasting bags or packs can be used, provided they are pierced to allow the steam to escape.

If using cling film, use that specifically designed for the microwave; conventional cling film should be avoided as the chemicals it contains may find their way into the food.

A range of white plastic cookware is now available, which lets virtually all the microwaves directly through to the food and absorbs back very little of the heat. Using these containers is likely to save an extra 20 per cent on cooking times.

**Glass, china and ceramic**  Heat-resistant glass bowls, casseroles and the like are ideal for microwave cooking. Ordinary glass utensils are unsuitable for lengthy cooking or to cook foods with a high sugar or fat content; they will overheat and crack. Glazed china and ceramic dishes are also suitable. Contrary to the manufacturers' claims and those of other tipsters, this type of microwave cookware does heat up. So be warned! You must take particular care when removing the lid from a covered container in which food has been cooking, and where steam has been building up.

**Cotton and linen**  Cotton and linen napkins can be used for short heating spells such as warming the breads. But do check the material is 100 percent cotton or linen and that it does not contain any synthetic fibres.

**Paper**  Kitchen paper towels, greaseproof paper and cardboard are all suitable for use as cover for the foods that are likely to splatter over the walls of the oven. A paper cover is ideal for quick cooking such as reheating or defrosting foods with a low sugar or fat and water content.

**Wicker and wood**  For short cooking or reheating purposes, containers made of wicker or wood can be used provided they do not contain metal wire, staples or glue-bonding. Wooden spoons can also be left in the microwave for short periods; afterwards, their moisture will dry out and they will crack.

**Browning skillet/dish**  The browning skillet (popular sizes are 8 inches and 10 inches across) was originally created to brown meat. It looks like other covered dishes, with one exception: its underside has a special coating similar to that on non-stick pans in conventional cooking. This coating absorbs the microwave energy, allowing the bottom of the dish to reach high temperatures and retain the heat for a considerable length of time.

Exercise great caution when removing the skillet from the oven, and make sure that it is placed on a heat-resistant surface. Follow the manufacturer's instructions for its cleaning and maintenance. Since browning has tremendous significance for Indian food, your browning skillet is a precious appliance.

Some microwaves now have a browning facility built into them, so one could be forgiven for thinking that the browning skillet is on its way out. However, millions of homes still have older models. Clearly therefore the browning skillet will be here for a while longer!

## OTHER UTENSILS

The preparation of dishes given herein sometimes requires typically Indian utensils and appliances which not every reader will be familiar with. These are used outside the microwave:

**Chakla-belan** A wooden breadboard and rolling pin, used for rolling out thin rounds of dough and pastry.

**Jhanna** A metal spoon with a long handle, and a perforated disc at the end. It is used for draining foods before they are taken out of the cooking vessel, or for making batter drops and faaluda.

**Kaddu-kas** A grater, used for many varieties of thin and thick gratings. Kaddu-kas come in various frames and shapes.

**Khalla-musaria** Also known as imaamdusta-aur daanti. Made of cast iron, clay or enamel, it roughly equates with the pestle and mortar. It comes in various shapes and sizes and is used for pounding hard ingredients.

**Sil-batta** A pair of treated stones, used for grinding herbs and spices. The ingredients are first placed over the sil – a large stone slab with a rough surface – and then pressed with the batta – the small round stone, also with a rough surface.

## WEIGHTS AND MEASURES

Traditionally, the experienced cooks of India do not normally talk in terms of exact weights and measures when they prepare dishes; they usually guess the quantities of ingredients to be used and invariably get first-class results. But until you gain some experience and expertise, it would only be proper to follow specific quantities of ingredients for all recipes.

However, because exact conversions of measurements (metric, Imperial and American) do not always result in convenient working quantities, the conversion figures given in this book are approximate and generally have been rounded off. Follow only one set of measurements when preparing a recipe as they are not interchangeable.

It is also imperative that you find your own level of acceptance for some of the strong ingredients first, then adapt the quantities to your taste. The most important in this regard are: chillies, ginger, garlic, sugar, salt, sugar syrup, ready-gravy and whole or powdered spices. To that extent, the weights and measures of these ingredients given in the recipes are for your general guidance only.

### Solid Weights

| Imperial | Metric |
|---|---|
| 1oz | 25g |
| 2oz | 50g |
| 3oz | 75g |
| 4oz (1/4lb) | 100g |
| 6oz | 175g |
| 8oz (1/2lb) | 225g |
| 16oz (1lb) | 450g |
| 18oz | 500g |
| 20oz (11/4lb) | 575g |
| 35oz | 1,000g (1kg) |

### Liquid Measures

| Imperial | Metric |
|---|---|
| 2 tablespoons (1fl oz) | 30ml |
| ¼ pint/10 tbspns (5fl oz) | 150ml |
| ½ pint (10fl oz) | 300ml |
| 1 pint (20fl oz) | 600ml |
| 1¾ pints (30fl oz) | 1,000ml (1l) |

### Spoon Measures

| 1 teaspoon | = | 1 teaspoon (5ml) |
|---|---|---|
| 1 dessertspoon | = | 1½ teaspoons |
| 1 tablespoon | = | 3 teaspoons (15ml) |

### Spoon and Cup Measures

| British | American |
|---|---|
| 1 teaspoon | 1 teaspoon |
| ¼ pint | ⅔ cup |
| ½ pint | 1¼ cups |
| 1 pint | 2½ cups |

### Some Assorted Measures

| Metric/Imperial | American |
|---|---|
| 225g/8oz ghee, sugar, rice, entils, fresh corn | 1 cup |
| 12 tablespoons ghee, oil, sugar, yoghurt | 1 cup |
| 100g/4oz most flours, batter-drops (boondi), dried peas, arrowroot, chopped nuts | 1 cup |
| 75g/3oz desiccated coconut | 1 cup |
| 175g/6oz green peas, semolina | 1 cup |

# Glossary of Ingredients

SAAMAGRIYON KA SHABDKOSH

**Almond** (*baadaam*)
A nut used in sweetmeats; rich in iron and proteins.

**Aniseed** (*patlee saunf*)
Used whole or ground. An appetizer and an aromatic, liquorice flavoured spice; served at the end of a meal, and used for making cordials.

**Asafoetida** *(heeng)*
A strong digestive spice, obtained from a kind of gum resin; has a powerful smell.

**Aubergine/Eggplant** (*baigan*)
A vegetable, rich in iron. It comes in long shapes, usually prepared stuffed (*bharwaan*); also available in bulbous round/oblong shapes, called 'brinjal' (bhaanta), which is best for mash (*bhurta*) preparation.

**Baking powder** (*khaane ka soda*)
A raising agent, used in pastries, batters and some bread preparations (*eg naan*); also known as bicarbonate of soda and baking soda.

**Banana** *(kela)*
A vegetable/fruit. Green ones used as vegetable and in other savouries; ripe ones used in puddings and raitas – rich in vitamins.

**Batter drops** *(boondi)*
Made from gram flour and water into a batter, which is then dropped and deep fried in ghee or oil. The little batter drops are then dried and stored in an airtight container and used to make sweets, raitas and 'kadhi'.

**Bay leaf** *(tej patta)*
An aromatic herb, used fresh or dried for flavouring vegetable and meat dishes.

**Beetroot** *(chukandar)*
A bulbous, dark red root that is eaten as a vegetable; also used in pickles and salads.

**Black beans** *(urad daal)*
These pulses can be whole or split, with their skin on, or hulled. Like other daals, they are also cooked usually into a purée.

Ground, wet or dry, urad daal is used in the preparation of many savoury dishes, and for stuffing.

**Black peppercorns** *(kaali/gol mirch)*
Said to be the first spice discovered by man; used whole or ground.

**Butter** *(makkhan)*
A fat rich in vitamins A and D; used to make ghee, or in making many sweet and savoury dishes.

**Butter milk** *(mattha)*
A refreshing, mildly sour liquid obtained by churning skimmed milk; used for making cold drinks and curried dishes.

**Cabbage** *(bundgobhi)*
A vegetable, low in calories – of the cauliflower family; rich in vitamin C.

**Cape gooseberries** *(rasbhari)*
Also known as Chinese lantern. A papery shell encases a golden berry. It tastes tart and has tiny seeds. It is ripe when the papery husk turns straw coloured.

**Capsicum** *(shimla mirch)*
Also known as green pepper. Rich in vitamin C; cooked stuffed, curried or with other ingredients.

**Cardamom, brown** *(bari ilaaichi)*
A scented spice, used in most vegetable and meat dishes. Larger than green cardamoms.

**Cardamom, green** *(chhoti ilaaichi)*
Buy in pods or as whole or ground seeds. A fragrant and digestive spice; used in many sweets and savouries, also served at the end of a meal.

**Carom seeds** *(ajwaain)*
Also known as 'thymol' or omum seeds; used in pickles, vegetables and savouries.

**Carrot** *(gaajar)*
A vegetable root, rich in vitamin A; good for the eyesight.

**Cashew nuts** *(kaaju)*
Used in pullaos, biriyanis and sweetmeats; rich in proteins and vitamin B.

**Cauliflower** *(gobhi)*
A vegetable, rich in vitamins and calcium.

**Celery** *(ajwaain patta)*
The leaf stalks of an umbelliferous plant, used in salads, vegetables and other savouries.

**Chapati flour** *(roti ka aata)*
Sustaining and wholesome starch obtained usually from wheat or other grains.

**Chilli, green** *(hari mirch)*
Used fresh or dried. Lends a hot, spicy flavour to food. If preferred, the seeds may be removed before using or serving.

**Chilli, red** *(laal mirch)*
The single hottest spice; used fresh or dried as well as in powder form as cayenne pepper. After preparing fresh chillies, wash your hands and never allow the volatile oils to touch your eyes or face, or anywhere else! Use sparingly.

**Chironji nuts** *(chiraunji)*
Also known as 'charauli'; used in puddings, pullaos and several other dishes

**Cinnamon** *(daal cheeni)*
Available in stick or powder form; used in curries, pullaos and sweetmeats.

**Cloves** *(laung)*
These dried flower buds can be bought whole or ground; used in sweets, savouries, spice powders and pickles.

**Coconut** *(gari/gola/naariyal)*
Used grated, fresh and dried for making sweets and savouries; the milk from its shell is widely used (called coconut milk).

**Coriander/Cilantro leaves** *(hara dhaniya)*
An aromatic herb, generally used for flavouring and garnishing.

**Coriander/Cilantro seeds** *(dhaniya ke beej)*
Used whole or ground; they have a light, fragrant, slightly lemony taste and are essential in most ground spice mixtures.

**Cornflour/Cornstarch** *(makke da aata)*
A thickening agent; used for breads and pastries.

**Cream cheese** *(chhena/paneer)*
Made from milk. Rich in vitamins B and D.

**Cucumber** *(kheera/kakdee)*
A cooling long green vegetable; used in raitas and sandwiches.

**Cumin seeds, black** *(kaala zeera)*
Also known as 'shaah' (royal) or 'siyaah' (black or dark) zeera. Distinguished from ordinary cumin by its smaller, dark seeds.

**Cumin seeds, white** *(sufeid zeera)*
Used whole or ground for flavouring and sautéeing. An essential ingredient of spice powders.

**Curry leaves** *(meethi neem)*
An aromatic leaf, used green or dry for flavouring.
**Curry powder** *(garam masaala)*
See garam masala.
**Dry dates** *(chhuhaara)*
An iron-rich fruit, used in 'sonth', sweetmeats, sauces and pickles.
**Dried milk** *(khoya)*
A preparation made from milk or milk powder with water; used
extensively in sweet dishes and some savoury dishes too. Khoya
can also be bought in block form from selected Asian grocers.
**Dry red chillies** *(sookhi laal mirch)*
Adds a spicy kick to savoury dishes. See also other 'chilli' entries.
**Fennel** *(moti saunf)*
Buy as vegetable or seeds; aniseed flavoured. Seeds often served
roasted, as an after-dinner refresher; also used in stuffing and in
pickles.
**Fenugreek leaves** *(methi ka saag)*
Used for making 'dry' vegetable dishes; rich in vitamin C.
A popular leafy vegetable, considered to be a great delicacy.
**Fenugreek seeds** *(methi daana)*
Yellow seeds with a strong curry flavour; used in pickles, whole or
ground.
**Flour, plain** *(maidaa)*
Starch used in breads, savouries and sweetmeats. Obtained from
white wheat grain.
**Garam masala** *(garam masaala)*
A mixture of a few hot spices; adds life and flavour to Indian
curries and savouries. Can be purchased ready-prepared in
packets.
**Garlic** *(lahsun)*
A bulbous herb with individual segments called 'cloves'; has a
strong pungent flavour.
**Ghee/clarified butter** *(ghee)*
An expensive but traditional cooking fat of India; made from butter.
**Ginger** *(taazi adrak)*
Buy dried or fresh root, or powdered; fresh is usually grated after
peeling. Adds flavour and has digestive properties.
**Gold foil** *(sonay ka warq)*
An edible thin foil, used for decorating sweet dishes, pullaos and
biriyanis; aids digestion.

**Gram, brown** *(bhoora chana)*
A very useful grain, rich in protein; used in curries, pickles and other savouries.

**Gram flour** *(besan)*
Gram flour is obtained by roasting and grinding the grams; it is a binding agent; used extensively for making 'pakodas', breads and batter.

**Grapes** *(angoor)*
Small, round fruit, with a purple or green skin and sweet flesh; can be eaten raw, or dried to make raisins or sultanas.

**Green mango** *(kachcha aam)*
Available as fruit (when ripe); for chutneys and pickles (when green); or dried pieces or powder (as aamchoor) for flavouring and souring.

**Green mung beans, dried** *(moong ki daal)*
A protein-rich legume; used for making purées, 'khichdee' and breads.

**Guava** *(amrood)*
A delicious fresh and fragrant fruit, eaten with its seeds; made into chutneys and salads. Can also be purchased in cans.

**Home-made cheese** *(chhena/paneer)*
See cream cheese.

**Honey** *(shahad)*
The sweet, thick fluid collected by bees from flowers; comes in many refinements.

**Ice creams** *(qulfiyaan)*
Cooling sweet preparations, made with milk, fruits and nuts.

**Jaggery** *(gur)*
Unrefined cane sugar, also known as molasses; used for making chutneys and in pickles. Being less sweet than sugar, quantities used are larger.

**Kewra essence** *(kewda arq)*
A concentrate of fragrance. See kewra water below.

**Kewra water** *(kewda jal)*
A liquid made from the flowers of 'kewda' plant (pandanus). Adds fragrance to puddings, cold drinks, 'qulfis' and rice preparations. Concentrated kewra essence is also available in small phials.

**Legumes** *(daalein)*
Used for making purées and stuffings – an integral part of a vegetarian meal; very rich in protein.

**Lemon** *(neebu)*
Used for souring; rich in vitamin C.

**Lentils** *(masoor ki daal)*
Protein-rich pulse; used for puréeing and stuffing. A name also applied to pulses and legumes collectively.

**Lettuce leaves** *(salaad ke patte)*
Tender clump of leaves from a garden plant; used in salads and for serving some savouries.

**Lime paste, edible** *(khaane ka choona)*
Used for making the 'paan' dish; also used as a tenderizing agent.

**Loquats** *(lukaat)*
Small, yellow, edible plum-like fruit from an ornamental evergreen tree of Asia.

**Lotus puffs** *(makhaana)*
When lotus seeds are roasted, they puff up and you have makhaanas! Used in making puddings and savouries.

**Lotus stems** *(kamal kakdee)*
Also called 'bhasinda'. A cooling vegetable, used also in kebabs and cutlets; rich in vitamins and minerals.

**Lychee** *(leechee)*
A seasonal fleshy fruit, covered by an outer skin, and looking like a red bulb; used in sweet dishes and salads.

**Mace** *(jaavitri)*
The outer membrane of nutmeg, with similar taste; buy as blades or powder. Used in meat dishes and other savouries.

**Mango** *(aam)*
Used green and ripe; a fruit for making pickles and chutneys as well as sweet dishes.

**Mango powder** *(aamchoor)*
A souring and flavouring agent, made by grinding dried green mango slices.

**Marrow** *(lauki)*
A vegetable, rich in vitamins and minerals: cooked on its own, with pulses or into sweets.

**Melon seeds** *(chaar maghaz)*
Washed and peeled melon seeds are used in many sweet and savoury preparations, and drinks.

**Milk** *(doodh)*
A white liquid obtained from cows or buffaloes; rich in calcium, proteins and vitamins A and B.

**Milk dough** (*khoya/maawa*)
See dried milk.
**Mint leaves** (*podina ki patti*)
A herb, used fresh in chutneys, raitas; generally used for garnishing yoghurt based dishes.
**Molasses** (*gur*)
See jaggery.
**Mushroom, black** (*guchchhi*)
A vegetable, used for making pullaos and curries.
**Mushroom, white** (*kukurmutta*)
A kind of fungus vegetable, used like the black mushroom above.
**Mustard oil** (*sarson ka teil*)
A common cooking oil in southern and eastern India, also used for pickles. It has a pungent flavour.
**Mustard seeds** (*raai*)
They can be yellow or black, and are rich in vitamin D and manganese; a souring agent, used for making pickles, sauces and chutneys.
**Nigella** (*kalaunji*)
Black onion seeds, normally used whole. Used for stuffings, pickles and for some meat dishes.
**Nutmeg** (*jaaiphal*)
Use whole spice, and grate as needed – can be bought ready-ground. Used for flavourings and savouries.
**Oil** (*teil*)
A viscous liquid of edible or lubricating variety, with smooth sticky feel; obtained from various plants, mineral deposits, animal substances and by synthesis. Use a vegetable or nut/seed oil (eg mustard, ground nut, sesame, coconut, sunflower) for cooking dishes in this book.
**Okra** (*bhindi*)
A green vegetable, also known as lady-fingers; buy small and fresh, without any blemishes.
**Onion** (*pyaaz*)
A vegetable/herb, used as a thickening agent in curries; contains sulphur and vitamin D.
**Orange** (*mausami*)
Used in drinks and desserts. This fruit is rich in vitamins A and C.
**Pear** (*naashpaati*)
A sweet, gritty-textured, juicy fruit which has a globular base,

tapering towards the top; used in salads, chutneys and curries.

**Peas** *(hari matar)*
Protein-rich vegetable (in pods of pulse family); used in many curries or savouries.

**Pepper** *(kaali mirch)*
A spice which cools by perspiration. Also see black peppercorns.

**Pigeon peas** *(arhar/toor daal)*
A pulse. The most popular daal; rich in protein.

**Pineapple** *(anannas)*
Often served in drinks or salads; used as chunks or liquid; rich in vitamins A and C.

**Pistachios** *(pishtay)*
An expensive nut; used in puddings, sweets, ice creams and biriyanis.

**Pomegranate seeds** *(Anaar daana)*
Sharp seeds used in making pakodas and samosas, and for flavouring.

**Poppy seeds** *(khus khus)*
A protein-rich aromatic spice.

**Potato** *(aalu)*
A carbohydrate-rich vegetable with multifarious uses in food.

**Preserve** *(murabba)*
A specially made variety of the Indian sweetmeat range, which can be stored (preserved) over long periods.

**Pulses** *(daalein)*
See legumes.

**Pumpkin** *(kaddu)*
A vegetable cooked in curry or 'dry' form; rich in vitamins.

**Radish, white** *(sufeid mooli)*
Indians normally use the white variety of this tangy root; used for making 'dry' vegetables and salads.

**Rhubarb** *(rewat cheeni)*
Plants with long green and red acid-tasting edible leafstalks; usually eaten cooked and sweetened.

**Rice** *(chaawal)*
A popular grain, rich in carbohydrates; used in pullaos and biriyanis.

**Rice flour** *(chaawal ka aata)*
Obtained by grinding dry or soaked rice; used to make savouries, and also as a thickening agent.

**Rose water** *(gulaab jal)*
An aromatic liquid prepared from fresh rose petals; used for flavouring sweet dishes, also used for soaking saffron strands.

**Saffron** *(kesar/jaafraan)*
The most expensive spice. Obtained from the stigma of the crocus flower, grown in abundance in the Kashmir valley. Used for rich yellow colouring and flavouring. Melts quickly in warm water and is known as the king of spices. Take extreme care when cooking it on its own in microwave.

**Salt, black** *(kaala namak)*
Used in selected 'chaat' dishes, raitas and sauces.

**Satsuma** *(santara)*
An edible citrus fruit, similar in shape and appearance to an orange. It has separate segments; used for tea and side dishes. Rich in iron and vitamin C.

**Silver foil, edible** *(chaandi ka warq)*
A digestive edible foil; normally used for decorating sweet and savoury dishes.

**Spinach** *(paalak)*
Green vegetable, rich in iron and calcium; contains vitamins A and C.

**Spring onion** *(hari pyaaz)*
Also called scallion. A seasonal green vegetable, used in salads and vegetable preparations; rich in vitamin C.

**Star fruit** *(kamrakh)*
Also known as carambola and babaco. When ripe, this large yellow rocket-shaped fruit (also regarded by some as a vegetable) with soft, juicy ribs; tastes exotically of strawberries and pineapple rolled into one.

**Sugar candy** *(misree)*
The ultimate form of sugar syrup. Served with roasted fennel seeds as a digestive after meals. Is available in packets at Indian grocers.

**Sugar syrup** *(chaashni)*
Made with sugar and water, and used extensively in sweet dishes.

**Sultanas/Golden raisins** *(kishmish)*
Iron-rich dry fruit, used in sweetmeats and puddings.

**Tamarind** *(imlee)*
A fruit, used in its green and ripe form, for making sauces and chutneys; a souring agent. Tamarind pulp and bottled concentrated tamarind sauce are available at Indian grocers. As either pulp or

concentrate it can be frozen in ice-cube trays and kept in the freezer for later use.

**Tomato** (*tamaatar*)

Used whole, chopped or puréed in large range of meats, vegetables, salads and chutneys. Rich in vitamins A, B, and C.

**Toor daal** *(arhar ki daal)*

See pigeon peas.

**Turmeric** *(huldi)*

Vivid yellow, powdered spice; use for colouring and flavouring; sometimes used as a substitute for saffron.

**Turnips** *(shaljum)*

A plant of mustard family with globular roots, rich in iron.

**Vermicelli** *(faaluda/semiyaan)*

Made from plain and other flours; used for making 'faaluda', to serve with 'qulfis' or in puddings, as seviyaan.

**Vinegar** *(sirka)*

A sour pickling agent, and a preservative. Used in sauces and savoury preparations.

**Water chestnuts** *(singhaara)*

Edible nut-like fruit, with two horn-like spikes, from a floating Asian aquatic plant. Used in making vegetables, salads, and its powder (flour) for making breads.

**White gourd** *(petha)*

A vegetable of the pumpkin family; normally used for making a particular sweetmeat of the same name – petha.

**Wholemeal/Wholewheat flour** *(roti ka aata)*

An unrefined (brown) starch for making wholesome bread dishes and savouries. Rich in fibre.

**Yeast** *(khameer)*

A fermentation agent, usually employed for raising dough.

**Yoghurt** *(dahee)*

A digestive milk product, used in numerous savoury dishes, curries, raitas and sweets.

# Jaadu ki Potlee

BASIC INGREDIENTS AND SPICES

*Over the centuries, the master chefs of India have experimented and developed techniques and a range of 'magical' basic ingredients – still largely unknown in the West – which are essentially responsible for the exoticism associated with Indian food.*

*These special preparations, when mixed with the other better known cookery ingredients, unleash a culinary chemistry which produces tantalizing tastes and fabulous flavours in food. Some of these ingredients, which make Indian cuisine unique and give it such an enviable reputation, are on offer here.*

*The cooking and preparation times given in this section are largely for your guidance only and may need to be slightly adjusted according to your personal preferences (in taste and appearance), the speed at which you work, the type and size of your microwave, and the state and temperature of the ingredients used.*

*Do feel free to experiment with alternatives, once you have gained some confidence in handling your microwave in the context of Indian food.*

# Aslee Ghee

## CLARIFIED BUTTER OR PURE GHEE

Makes 225 g/8 oz/1 cup

275 g/10 oz/1¼ cups
  unsalted butter

Prep 2 min
Cooking 10 min
+ standing time 5 min

*One of the magical basic recipes of Indian cuisine, ghee is the traditional and best medium of cooking Indian food. It is easy to make at home in your microwave. You can make larger amounts to keep in the kitchen for several weeks. Put it in the refrigerator for longer periods; it can be frozen, too.*

1. Cut the butter into small pieces, place in a microwave-safe bowl and cook, uncovered, for 2 minutes or until the butter has melted.
2. Cover the bowl and cook at full power for 8 minutes: there is no need to stir or keep a constant vigil. Near the end of cooking time, open the oven to check the butter and ensure that you switch off the oven when the liquid has boiled and turned light golden. After the initial spluttering, it will become quiet and eventually turn clear. The moisture has by now evaporated and the protein and impurities have settled at the bottom.
3. Remove the ghee from the oven and, while it is standing, use a wooden spatula to remove any scum from the top. Leave to stand for 5 minutes.
4. After the standing time, carefully strain the clear liquid into a covered container, discarding the residue at the bottom, and leave to cool. The ghee will set as it cools.

# Bhuna Pisaa Dhania

TOASTED CORIANDER POWDER

*Make small amounts of this powder at a time, in the interest of retaining the fresh aroma. It is used in most dry and curried vegetable and meat preparations.*

1. Pick and clean the seeds and spread them on a microwave-safe shallow dish. No greasing is required.
2. Toast, uncovered, at full power for 4 minutes. Stir a couple of times during cooking, and watch out for that aromatic smell and the changing colour of the seeds.
3. Let the coriander seeds stand and, when completely cool, grind to a fine powder. Store in a cool place in an airtight container. Close the lid tightly after each use.

**Makes 50 g/2 oz/½ cup**

**50 g/2 oz/1 cup coriander seeds**

**Prep 4 min**
**Cooking 4 min**
**+ standing time 5 min**

# Bhuna Zeera Masaala

TOASTED CUMIN POWDER

**Makes 2 tablespoons**

**2 tablespoons white cumin
seeds**

**Prep 4 min**
**Cooking 4 min**
**+ standing time 5 min**

*Freshly ground cumin has a strong, aromatic fragrance which begins to subside with time. This powder is used extensively in northern and central India to enhance the flavour of yoghurt and buttermilk-based dishes.*

1. Pick and clean the cumin seeds and put them on a plain, ungreased pie or dinner plate.
2. Toast, uncovered, at full power for 4 minutes, until the seeds give out a pungent smell and assume a darker hue. Stir once or twice during cooking, to prevent burning and uneven browning.
3. Let the seeds stand and cool completely. Grind coarsely (or finely, if preferred) and store in an airtight container. Make sure you close the lid of the container tightly after each use.

# Garam Masaala

MIXED SPICE POWDER

*Garam masaala is a mixture of several hot spices and is the vital ingredient for all the major Indian savoury dishes – curried, dry and braised. It is used at various stages of the cooking process. Most Indian chefs have their own recipe for this preparation. Although the powder will last for several weeks at room temperature, the pungency will fade as time goes on, so don't make too much at once.*

1. Mix all the ingredients together and spread them on a shallow microwave-friendly dish. Cook at full power for 8 minutes, stirring a couple of times during cooking to ensure even browning

2. When the spices give out a strong aroma and have turned several shades darker, remove from the oven and let them stand for 5 minutes.

3. When completely cool, grind the mixture to a fine powder. If an electric grinder is not available, grind the spices by hand on a sil-batta then push through a fine sieve or muslin cloth. Store in an airtight container.

**Makes 100 g/4 oz/1 cup**

4 tablespoons/⅓ cup
   coriander seeds
25 g/1 oz white cumin seeds
25 g/1 oz cloves
25 g/1 oz black peppercorns
1 tablespoon brown
   cardamom seeds
4 bay leaves, crushed
2 cinnamon sticks, each
   about 2½ cm/1 inch long,
   broken
pinch of grated nutmeg
pinch or blade of mace,
   crushed

**Prep 5 min**
**Cooking 8 min**
**+ standing time 5 min**

# Saambhar Masaala

## SAAMBHAR POWDER

**Makes 100 g/4 oz/1 cup**

2 tablespoons pigeon
peas/toor daal
2 tablespoons mustard seeds
4 tablespoons coriander
seeds
1 teaspoon fenugreek seeds
2 teaspoons black
peppercorns
1 tablespoon dry curry
leaves, crushed
8 dry red chillies, crushed
1 tablespoon white cumin
seeds
pinch of asafoetida powder
large pinch of turmeric
powder

**Prep 5 min**
**Cooking 6 min**
**+ standing time 2 min**

*This spice mixture, like garam masaala, varies a great deal between chefs. To make a mild version, reduce the quantities of chilli and pepper. Omit the turmeric if you do not like yellow-coloured food. Saambhar powder is primarily used to make vegetable stews and sauces that are served with south Indian dishes like dosa and wadaa.*

1. Mix all of the ingredients together and spread them out on a flat microwavable dish. Roast the mixture, uncovered, at full power for about 6 minutes, or until the spices begin to brown and give out a strong, aromatic smell. Stir once during cooking.
2. Remove the spice mixture from the oven and leave it to stand for 2 minutes. When completely cool, grind it into a fine powder and push through a muslin cloth or fine sieve if necessary.
3. Transfer the powder to an airtight container, in which it will last for several weeks, kept in a cool place. Close the lid tightly after each use.

# Tandoori Masaala

## TANDOOR POWDER

*Made from raw spices, this powder is responsible for imparting a superb exotic flavour to traditional tandoori dishes, which are made in a clay oven, or a substitute. It is particularly good for chicken, steak and tikka dishes. Use ready-made powders, or make your own and then blend them together.*

1. Mix all of the ingredients together then store the mixture in an airtight container. Close the lid tightly after each use.

Makes 50 g/2 oz/½ cup

2 tablespoons ground coriander powder
1½ teaspoons cumin powder
½ teaspoon ground nutmeg
1 teaspoon ground mace
1 teaspoon ground cloves
1 teaspoon ground pepper
1 teaspoon ground fenugreek
1 teaspoon ground cinnamon
1 teaspoon ground brown cardamom seeds
1 teaspoon garlic powder
1 teaspoon ground ginger
2 teaspoons red food colouring

Prep 10 min

# Vindaloo Masaala

## VINDALOO POWDER

**Makes 100 g/4 oz/1 cup**

**8 dry red chillies
1 tablespoon cloves
1 tablespoon black
   peppercorns
2 tablespoons mustard seeds
4 tablespoons
   coriander seeds
1 tablespoon fenugreek
   seeds
4 cinnamon sticks, each
   about 5 cm/2 inches long
1 tablespoon white cumin
   seeds
seeds of 4 brown cardamoms
8 bay leaves, crushed**

**Prep 10 min
Cooking 5 min
+ standing time 2 min**

*A hot powder from the Madras region for your favourite dishes such as mutton or duck vindaloo. Dare a little and use a spoonful of it over grilled dishes like fish, meat, hamburgers or hot dogs. It is sure to do wonders for your taste buds!*

1. Spread all the spices on a suitable dinner plate and roast at full power for 5 minutes, stirring a couple of times during cooking.
2. When the spices change colour and give out a pungent smell, remove them from the oven and leave to stand for 2 minutes.
3. When completely cool, grind into a fine powder then press the mixture through a fine muslin cloth or fine sieve. Store in an airtight container in a cool place.

# Namkeen Gutkay

SEASONED SIPPETS OR CROÛTONS

*Croûtons add muscle and style to soup dishes. When made in the microwave, the croûtons come out lighter and crisper. They can be made in advance and stored for several days. They last even longer when refrigerated, or frozen.*

1. Trim the bread slices and cut them into small cubes.
2. Take a microwave-friendly dinner plate and arrange the bread cubes on it. Lightly sprinkle the salt and pepper over the bread then pour a drop of oil over each piece.
3. Without covering, cook at full power for 3 minutes, turning the croûtons over once about halfway through cooking.
4. Remove and place on absorbent paper. Leave the croûtons to stand for 2 minutes then serve as directed or store in an airtight container.

**Serves 4**

2 thick slices bread
small pinch of salt
pinch of freshly ground
  pepper
1 tablespoon ghee or oil

**Prep 5 min**
**Cooking 3 min**
**+ standing time 2 min**

# Tadkaa Pyaaz

## CARAMELIZED ONIONS

**Serves 4**

2 tablespoons ghee or oil
3 tablespoons/¼ cup finely
   sliced onion

Prep 2 min
Cooking 5 min
+ standing time 2 min

*The primary purpose of all tadkaa preparations is to perk up a bland dish and thereby tickle the taste buds. They offer visual attraction as well as contrast in texture. This one is often served with khichdee, daal and pullao dishes. Use freshly made tadkaa pyaaz wherever possible.*

1. Heat the oil at full power for 2 minutes in a microwavable lidded flat dish or skillet.
2. Remove the lid, stir the onion into the oil and cook, uncovered, at full power for 3 minutes or until the onion is opaque or brown to the shade of your preference. Watch the onion carefully: after losing moisture, it frazzles rather quickly.
3. Use immediately to garnish the dish, on which it should stand for 2 minutes before serving.

# Zeera Ka Tadkaa

## SAUTÉED CUMIN

**The role of this tadkaa is the same, ie to enhance the taste and texture of bland dishes. Prepare it with a mixture of onions, if preferred.**

1. Place the ghee or oil in a covered dish or skillet and heat at full power for 1 minute.
2. Add the cumin and stir well. Cook, uncovered, at full power for 3 minutes. Stir once or twice during cooking.
3. When the cumin turns dark, switch off the oven and immediately pour the cumin over the dish with which it is to be served. Leave to stand for 2 minutes before serving.

Serves 4

2 tablespoons melted ghee
  or oil
2 tablespoons white cumin
  seeds

Prep 2 min
Cooking 4 min
+ standing time 2 min

# Raai Ka Tadkaa

GLAZED MUSTARD

**Serves 4**

2 tablespoons melted ghee or
  oil
2 tablespoons whole yellow
  mustard seeds

**Prep 2 min**
**Cooking 4 min**
**+ standing time 2 min**

*Other than with the usual type of dishes, this tadkaa is particularly good served with kadhee and some savoury snacks like a daal moth or chanaa murmuraa.*

1. Take a covered casserole or skillet and heat the ghee or oil in it at full power for 2 minutes.
2. Remove from the oven, add the mustard and immediately replace the lid. Cook at full power for 2 minutes or until the mustard starts to splutter.
3. Pour the mustard at once over the food with which it is to be served. Let it stand for 2 minutes before serving.

# *Taaza Shorwaa - Shaakahaari*

## Vegetarian Ready Gravy

*This gravy can be used to curry-up dry dishes or in any recipes requiring ready gravy. To store long term, freeze the liquid in ice cubes, then transfer to plastic bags and keep in the freezer.*

1. Place the ghee and onion in a 1.2 litre/2 pint/5 cup lidded casserole and cook, covered, at full power for 3 minutes.
2. Stir in the garlic, ginger, turmeric, chilli and coriander and continue cooking, covered, for another 2 minutes.
3. Add the tomato purée and yoghurt and cook, covered, at full power for another 3 minutes. Stir a couple of times during cooking.
4. Pour in the water and salt, lower the heat to medium and cook, covered, for a further 12 minutes. Remove from the oven and leave to stand and cool.
5. When cool, purée the mixture using a blender or food processor. Strain and use immediately; alternatively, store the gravy in a covered container in the refrigerator for up to 2 days, or freeze for up to 3 months.

Makes 300 ml/½ pint/1¼ cups

100 g/4 oz/½ cup ghee
1 large onion, finely chopped
2 cloves garlic, crushed
½ teaspoon grated root ginger
1 teaspoon turmeric powder
1 teaspoon red chilli powder
1 tablespoon ground coriander
2 tablespoons tomato purée
2 tablespoons plain yoghurt
300 ml/½ pint/1¼ cups warm water
½ teaspoon salt

Prep 10 min
Cooking 20 min
+ standing time 5 min

# Taaza Shorwaa - Maansahaari

MEAT OR CHICKEN READY GRAVY

Makes 600 ml/1 pint/2½ cups

100 g/4 oz/½ cup ghee
1 large onion, finely chopped
450 g/1 lb fleshy chicken or
   meat bones, cracked
2 cloves garlic, crushed
½ teaspoon grated root
   ginger
1 teaspoon turmeric powder
1 teaspoon red chilli powder
1 tablespoon ground
   coriander
2 tablespoons tomato purée
2 tablespoons plain yoghurt
600 ml/1 pint/2½ cups water
1 teaspoon salt
2 tablespoons garam masala

Prep 15 min
Cooking 20 min
+ standing time 5 min

*This spicy gravy can be used to flavour pullaos, biriyaanis and for making non-vegetarian curries. It helps to make large quantities in advance, frozen in cubes to use when required.*

1. Use a microwave-friendly 1.8 litre/3 pint/7½ cup lidded casserole. Add the ghee and onion and cook, covered, at full power for 3 minutes.
2. Stir in the bones, garlic, ginger, turmeric, chilli powder, coriander, tomato purée and yoghurt. Cook, covered, at full power for 2 minutes then stir thoroughly.
3. Add the water and salt and cook, covered, at full power for 15 minutes, stirring once halfway through cooking. Two minutes before the end of the cooking time, stir in the garam masala, re-cover and continue cooking.
4. Leave the mixture to stand and, when cool, strain and use immediately. Alternatively, store covered in the refrigerator for up to 2 days, or freeze in cubes.

# Khoyaa or Maawa

MILK DOUGH

*Most Indian sweetmeats are based on khoyaa. This magic ingredient brings out the spectacular in sweet dishes. It keeps in the refrigerator for about a month and can be frozen for longer periods.*

Makes 75 g/3 oz/¼ cup

600 ml/1 pint/2½ cups
  creamy milk

Prep 2 min
Cooking 35 min
+ standing time 5 min

1. Pour the milk into a 1.8 litre/3 pint/7½ cup capacity casserole or pan and cook, uncovered, for 10 minutes at full power. Stir a couple of times during cooking.
2. Reduce the power to medium and cook, uncovered, for another 25 minutes. Stir more often during this second phase.
3. When the milk has reduced to one-eighth of its original quantity and resembles a creamy pastry (and before it changes substantially in colour), remove it from the oven and leave to stand and cool.
4. Place the khoyaa in a covered container and refrigerate until required.

Variations: There are two alternative methods of making khoyaa. If you are short of time, you can make khoyaa by mixing 75g/3 oz/1 cup of whole milk powder with 2 table-spoons of creamy milk. Cook, uncovered, at full power for about 10 minutes, stirring a couple of times in between. This method will not beat the original, but it will do the job. Alternatively, there is a granular variety of khoyaa. Follow the first recipe, adding the juice of 2 lemons to the milk after it has been cooking for 10 minutes. The milk will coagulate. You should then proceed as in the original recipe. The resultant granular khoyaa is particularly stylish and suitable for making the kalaakand variety of burfi. Serve the burfi bedecked with silver foil.

# Chhena aur Paneer

## HOME-MADE CREAM CHEESE

Makes 100 g/4 oz/½ cup

600 ml/1 pint/2½ cups whole
  creamy milk
juice of ½ lemon, or 1
  tablespoon vinegar or plain
  yoghurt

Prep 10 min + setting time
Cooking 10 min
+ standing time 5 min

*Chhena and paneer are made from the same basic recipe. While chhena is the base for many popular mouth-watering sweetmeats, paneer is mostly used for making curries and other savoury dishes.*

1. Place the milk in a microwave-safe casserole or pan with a capacity of 1.8 litres/3 pints/7½ cups. Cook, uncovered, at full power for 10 minutes. Stir once during cooking to break the skin forming on the surface.
2. Remove the dish from the oven and stir the milk for about 5 minutes until cool. Add the lemon juice (or vinegar or yoghurt, if using) and keep stirring until the milk coagulates.
3. Line a sieve with a clean muslin cloth and pour the curdled milk through it. Draw the corners of the muslin together to make a bag and gently squeeze out the liquid. The curds remaining in the cloth are chhena, which can be used immediately or stored in the refrigerator.
4. To make paneer, mould the chhena into a block and press it under a heavy weight until it sets – this should take about an hour.
5. Cut the set paneer into square or diamond shapes as desired, then place it in a covered dish and store in the refrigerator.

# Chaashni

SUGAR SYRUP

*Sugar syrup is used in the preparation of many Indian sweetmeats. This basic recipe includes instructions for different strengths of syrup. Traditionally, a large amount of sugar is used: adjust the quantity to your level of acceptance.*

**Makes 150 ml/¼ pint/⅔ cup**

600 ml/1 pint/2½ cups water
2 tablespoons milk
450 g/1 lb/2 cups sugar

**Prep 5 min**
**Cooking 10 min**
**+ standing time 5 min**

1. Pour all the ingredients into a microwave-safe 1.2 litre/ 2 pint/5 cup glass measure and stir thoroughly. Cook at full power, uncovered, for 5 minutes or until the mixture comes to a boil. Stir once during cooking.

2. Remove the container from the oven and skim any scum that has formed on the top of the syrup. Lower the power of the oven to medium and cook the syrup for another 5 minutes. Skim the surface a couple more times during this phase of cooking.

3. When the syrup has cooked, test it by pinching some between your thumb and forefinger: if a drop of syrup lifts up in one string, it is known as one-string syrup. This strength of syrup is adequate for most sweets. You may continue cooking the mixture in order to make a 2, 3 or 4-string syrup. Eventually the syrup will crack into chips, forming sugar candy (*misree*); this is sold ready-made at Asian grocers.

# Bhojan ka Sriganesh

HORS D'OEUVRES

Indian cuisine has an inexhaustible store of starters, snacks and quick dishes. Very many of them can be made easily and fairly quickly. However, when using the microwave, you cannot deep-fry: that rules out a large chunk of traditional dishes in this category and I have thus had to be selective. I hope my choice meets with your approval.

It is important to be mindful at all times that food continues to cook even after it has been taken out of the oven. That is why standing times are desirable for most dishes. It is so easy to overcook, particularly dishes containing eggs or cheese; they then become hard and rubbery. It is best therefore to undercook until you are sure, so that if a dish, after the standing time, still looks undercooked, you can easily cook a little more.

# Paapad

POPPADUMS

Serves 4

4 poppadums, halved

Prep 2 min
Cooking 2 min
+ standing time 2 min

*Poppadums are a specialty of Indian cuisine and are made from lentils, grams, rice or potatoes. The varieties of poppadum are many – from paper-thin to quite thick, from bland to blazing hot. Serve them with soup as a light meal, or as a starter or side dish with main meals. A poppadum toasts more evenly in the microwave (and with no added calories) than if deep-fried or roasted on hot charcoal.*

1. Arrange the poppadum halves on a flat dish and microwave on full power for 1 minute.
2. Turn over and cook on the other side, at the same level of heat, for another minute.
3. Stand for 2 minutes until the poppadum hardens then serve hot, warm or cold.

# Garam Bhuttay

CORN-ON-THE-COB

*This dish is economical, quick and delicious. It is popular with young and old, rich and poor alike and makes a good snack or starter.*

1. Peel the husks from the corn cobs and remove the silky hairs. In a small bowl, blend together the butter and garlic and rub the mixture all over the cobs.
2. Wrap the cobs loosely in greaseproof paper or put the husks back on. Place the cobs side by side on a shallow dish and microwave on full power for 12 minutes. Turn over a couple of times during cooking.
3. Take a lemon half, dip it in salt and pepper and rub it over a cooked cob, squeezing the lemon all the time. Repeat with the remaining cobs. Leave to stand for 4 minutes then serve hot.

Serves 4

4 small corn-on-the-cobs, peeled
50 g/2 oz/¼ cup butter, softened
2 cloves garlic, crushed, or ½ teaspoon garlic powder
2 juicy lemons, halved
salt and pepper

Prep 10 min
Cooking 12 min
+ standing time 4 min

# Hari Dhaniya Ke Aalu

POTATO IN GREEN CORIANDER

Serves 4

4 medium potatoes
4 tablespoons coriander
  leaves
1 teaspoon salt, or to taste
4 green chillies
2 tablespoons lemon juice

Prep 15 min
Cooking 5 min
+ standing time 5 min

*This is a chaat dish which can appropriately be served as a starter, tea-time snack or as a side dish with the main meal. It is economical, quick to make and tastes out of this world! Adjust the quantity of ingredients in the paste to suit your taste.*

1. Wash, scrub and dry the potatoes, then prick them all over with a fork.
2. Place the potatoes on absorbent paper in the microwave and cook on full power for 5 minutes or until soft when gently squeezed. Turn them over once during cooking.
3. Leave the potatoes to stand for 5 minutes, or dip them into cold water, before peeling off the skin. Cut each potato into 4 or 6 pieces.
4. Grind the coriander leaves, salt, chillies and lemon juice together to make a paste. Smear this paste thickly over the potato pieces and leave them for 2 minutes to soak in the flavour.
5. Serve cold and eat with cocktail sticks or spoons.

# Chatpatee Baiganee

## FRISKY AUBERGINE FRITTERS

**These apparently ordinary fritters assume quite scrumptious dimensions when served smothered in tamarind sauce and condiments. You may also serve them without sauce.**

1. Make a batter using the flour, water and powder mix.
2. Heat the oil in a covered skillet at full power for 3 minutes. Remove the skillet from the oven, dip the aubergine slices in batter and place them in the oil. Put the lid back on and return the skillet to the oven; cook for 3 minutes.
3. Turn over the slices of aubergine then cook for another 3 minutes.
4. Remove the aubergine slices from the oven and put them on a serving dish. Leave to stand for 5 minutes.
5. Meanwhile, place the tamarind cubes and condiments of your choice in a covered casserole and cook at full power for 3 minutes or until the sauce boils. Remove from the oven, pour over the fritters and serve hot. You may serve them later, after reheating.

Serves 4

100 g/4 oz/1 cup gram flour (besan)
150 ml/¼ pint/⅔ cup water
50 g/2 oz/½ cup mixture of rice and black bean (urad) powders
2 tablespoons cooking oil
2 small aubergines/eggplants, sliced lengthways
6 tamarind cubes (see p. 21)
condiments such as plain and black salts, cumin powder, red chilli powder

Prep 10 min
Cooking 12 min
+ standing time 5 min

# Aalu Pakora or Bhajia

POTATO PAKORA

Serves 4

100 g/4 oz/1 cup gram flour
  (besan)
pinch of bicarbonate of soda
150 ml/¼ pint/⅔ cup water
1 teaspoon salt, or to taste
1 teaspoon red chilli powder
4 medium potatoes
2 tablespoons cooking oil

Prep 15 min
+ resting time
Cooking 9 min
+ standing time 5 min

*Indian pakora needs no introduction. Do adapt the consistency of the batter and the chilli content to your level of acceptance but remember this will affect the cooking times. The more adventurous among you may wish to experiment with alternative main ingredients – may I suggest onion rings, egg slices or fish fillets.*

1. Put the flour and soda in a bowl and gradually add the water to make a smooth batter. Stir in the salt and chilli and whisk thoroughly. Leave to rest for 15 minutes.
2. Cut the potatoes into thin round slices. Don't leave them unused for long or they will turn dark brown or black. If you do not want to cook them straightaway, leave the slices in water with a pinch of salt.
3. Take a covered skillet and heat the oil at full power for 3 minutes. Remove from the oven and open the lid. Dip each potato slice in batter then place it in the oil.
4. Replace the lid and return the skillet to the oven. Cook at full power for 3 minutes then turn over the potato slices and continue cooking for another 3 minutes.
5. Remove the skillet from the oven and transfer the pakoras to some absorbent paper. Leave to stand for 5 minutes and serve with a chutney of your choice.

# Moong Ki Daalmoth

TASTY GREEN BEANS

*A splendid daalmoth dish indeed. It is easy to make (although the beans have to be soaked overnight) and can be stored for later use. Serve hot or cold, as desired, with tea or drinks, or as a starter or snack.*

1. Wash and soak the beans overnight. Next day, drain off the water and let the beans dry completely.
2. Heat the oil in a lidded skillet at full power for 3 minutes. Then remove it from the oven and stir in the beans.
3. Cover and cook at full power for 6 minutes, stopping to stir halfway through cooking and adjusting the time according to your taste and the size of the oven.
4. When the beans have finished cooking, transfer them to some absorbent paper and leave to stand until the beans are cool and completely dry.
5. Place the beans in a bowl and stir in the salt, mango powder and pepper. If you want to spike your taste buds, use cayenne instead of pepper. Store the beans in an airtight container and use when required.

Serves 8

225 g/8 oz/½ lb skinless,
  split green beans
2 tablespoons cooking oil
salt to taste
pinch of mango powder
large pinch of ground pepper
  or cayenne

Prep 10 min
+ soaking time
Cooking 9 min
+ cooling time

# Bhuna Paneer Masaala

## CREAM-CHEESE SAVOURY CHUNKS

Serves 4

1 block paneer (see p.38)
1 tablespoon oil
salt and pepper
1 teaspoon lemon juice

Prep 5 min
Cooking 4 min
+ standing time 2 min

*In Indian cooking, home-made cheese is a many-splendoured thing. It can be made in advance and used in sweet and savoury dishes. This starter can be made very quickly and goes down a treat.*

1. Cut the cheese into 16 large chunks.
2. Heat half the oil in a covered skillet at full power for 2 minutes. Remove from the oven and add the cheese. Dribble the remaining oil over the cheese, cover with the lid, return to the oven and cook for 1 minute.
3. Turn the chunks of cheese over, replace the lid and cook for a further minute.
4. Place the chunks on a serving dish and leave to stand for 2 minutes. Sprinkle with the seasonings and lemon juice and serve with cocktail sticks. If you want to be a little more formal, serve the cheese chunks on a bed of lettuce, surrounded by chunks of pineapple, sliced onion and potato wafers.

# *Pagay Chilghozay*

CARAMELIZED PINE NUTS

*Although pine nuts are specified for this dish, you may wish to experiment with alternatives such as almonds, walnuts and pistachios. Stored in an airtight container, they will last for several days, even weeks*

1. Spread the pine nuts on a dinner plate and roast, uncovered, for 2 minutes at full power. Stir once halfway through cooking. Remove from the oven and set aside.
2. Place the sugar, water, ghee, soda and saffron in a microwave-safe bowl. Cook for 3 minutes, uncovered, or until the syrup is of a thick liquid consistency.
3. Remove the syrup from the oven, sprinkle with salt and pepper and stir once or twice. Then add the nuts and mix rapidly.
4. Leave the mixture to stand. During this time it will begin to dry up: make sure the nuts are not clinging together. Serve when cool, or store for later use.

Serves 4

100 g/4 oz/1 cup pine nuts
50 g/2 oz/¼ cup sugar
2 tablespoons water
1 teaspoon ghee (see p.24)
pinch of bicarbonate of soda
4-6 saffron strands
salt and pepper

Prep 5 min
Cooking 5 min
+ standing time 2 min

# Memna Kabaab

## LAMB SAUCERS

Serves 4

450 g/1 lb minced lamb
½ teaspoon poppy seeds
4 green chillies, chopped
5 cm/2 inch piece root ginger
4 cloves garlic, chopped
1 medium onion, chopped
1 tablespoon garam masaala
2 teaspoons salt
2 slices bread
50 g/2 oz/½ cup gram flour
   (besan)
1 tablespoon ghee
2 tablespoons chopped
   coriander
oil or butter, for greasing
lettuce, to garnish

Prep 20 min
+ resting time
Cooking 9 min
+ standing time 5 min

*Feel free to fly away with these delicious saucers! They can be served hot or cold, as starter, snack or a side dish – they are particularly suitable for parties and picnics. East and West can meet cordially by serving the patties in buns as burgers – children will love it. You may use other meats for this dish too.*

1. Place the mince, poppy seeds, chillies, ginger, garlic, onion, garam masaala and salt in a grinder and grind finely, or use a sil-batta. Let the mixture rest for 20 minutes.
2. Fold in the bread, gram flour (besan), ghee and coriander and knead the mixture together. Divide it into eight portions and make saucer-shaped discs using the greased palms of your hands.
3. Put the patties on a greased shallow dish and microwave on full power for 9 minutes. Turn over halfway through cooking.
4. Serve hot, if preferred, on a bed of lettuce or similar garnish with a chutney or sauce of your choice.

# Masaaledaar Murghee

SPICY CHICKEN WINGS

*This is a tandoori-style preparation which also is known as tangdee kabaab. With this dish you will always delight your discriminating guests and establish your culinary dexterity. Adjust the masaala, oil and lemon to your taste.*

1. Prick the chicken wings carefully with a fork and smear the yoghurt all over them. Marinade overnight, or for at least 4 hours.

2. In a small bowl, make a paste from the tandoori masaala, oil, lemon juice and a little salt. Rub it generously all over the wings. Leave to stand for 1 hour to marinate further.

3. Break the eggs into a medium-sized bowl and beat them with the cornflour to make a batter. Dip each wing into the batter and then roll it in the breadcrumbs.

4. Arrange the wings in a circle on a flat ovenproof dish, placing the thinner ends towards the centre of the dish and the fleshy parts outwards. Microwave on full power for 15 minutes, or until juices run clear when the chicken is pierced with the tip of a knife. Turn over halfway through cooking.

5. Leave the chicken wings to stand for 5 minutes then serve with a squeeze of lemon and a sour chutney of your choice.

Serves 4

8 chicken wings, skinned
100 g/4 oz/½ cup plain yoghurt
4 tablespoons/⅓ cup tandoori masaala
2 teaspoons cooking oil
2 tablespoons lemon juice
salt
4 eggs
2 tablespoons cornflour
breadcrumbs, for coating

Prep 20 min
+ marinating time
Cooking 15 min
+ standing time 5 min

# Murghee Choochi Tikka

SPICY CHICKEN BREAST

**Serves 4**

4 chicken breasts, skinned
300 ml/½ pint/1¼ cups
  plain yoghurt
2 cloves of garlic
2 teaspoons grated root
  ginger
1 tablespoon sliced onion
1 green chilli, finely chopped
1 teaspoon ground cumin
1 tablespoon lemon juice
2 tablespoons chopped
  coriander, or mint leaves
salt

**Prep 10 min**
**+ marinating time**
**Cooking 6 min**
**+ standing time 4 min**

*Boneless pieces of meat, when spiced up and dry-roasted with a licking of ghee or oil, are called tikka. When cooking them in the microwave, it helps to have pieces of uniform thickness and size. I am sure this concoction will find favour with all chicken lovers.*

1. Cut the chicken breasts into small pieces or, if preferred, keep them whole and make shallow slashes all over with a knife, or prick them all over with a fork.
2. Take 6-8 tablespoons of the yoghurt and smear it all over the chicken and inside the gashes, if appropriate. Leave to marinate overnight or for at least 4 hours.
3. In a small bowl, make a paste from the garlic, ginger, onion, chilli, cumin, lemon juice and a pinch of salt. Smear this paste thickly all over the chicken pieces and leave to marinate on a plate.
4. Take a skillet or lidded shallow pan. Grease the surface and heat, uncovered, for 1 minute. Add the chicken, cover and cook on medium for 2 minutes. Turn over the chicken pieces and cook for another 3 minutes or until it is cooked to your taste – normally, if the juices run clear when the chicken is pierced with a fork or skewer, it is ready.
5. Leave the chicken to stand. Meanwhile, grind or finely mince the coriander or mint leaves and stir them into the remaining yoghurt to make a chutney. Add salt to taste and serve with the hot chicken.

# Jheenga Chaarmaghaz

PRAWNS STUDDED WITH MELON SEEDS

**A great favourite of the Bombay and Calcutta regions. Many variations are possible.**

1. Lightly grease a microwave-friendly plate and spread the melon seeds out on it. Cook, uncovered, for 2 minutes, stirring halfway through cooking. Remove from the oven and set aside.
2. Peel the prawns, wash them carefully and pat dry.
3. In a small bowl, make a paste using the garlic, onion, ginger, chilli powder, salt and cornflour and smear it over each of the prawns. Dip the prawns in the roasted melon seeds until thoroughly coated.
4. Grease the surface of a lidded skillet and arrange the spiced prawns on it. Cover and cook on full power for 3 minutes, turning over halfway through.
5. Leave the prawns to stand for 2 minutes then sprinkle them with the lemon juice and serve hot.

Serves 4

oil, for greasing
50 g/2 oz/½ cup melon seeds
225 g/8 oz/1/1¼ cups
    raw green prawns/shrimp
1 small clove garlic
1 teaspoon chopped onion
½ teaspoon grated root
    ginger
pinch of red chilli powder
pinch of salt
½ teaspoon cornflour
lemon juice, to serve

Prep 10 min
Cooking 5 min
+ standing time 2 min

# Shorway

SOUPS AND APPETIZERS

*Gone are the days when soup-making took many hours. Microwave culture has changed all that. There is no need to plan them in advance and they last for several days in the refrigerator.*

*Soups can be thick or thin, piping hot or chilled. They should be cooked in deep, round containers and you should always leave room for the liquid to expand as it begins to boil. Reheating is normally done at full power and the average timings are: two minutes for 225 ml/8 floz/1 cup, five minutes for 900 ml/1½ pints/4 cups and eight minutes for 2.2 litres/3 ½ pints/9 cups. Stir at least once in order to ensure even heating.*

*The soup course is something of a gate-crasher on the traditional Indian gastronomic scene. Indians do not drink soups per se with their meals, even today. A need for soups arose when British army officers stationed in India insisted on a traditional appetizer before their main meal.*

*Indians have always drunk shorwaas in the north and rasams in the south – juices from cooking legumes, rice, vegetables and meats. These lead to some thin, clear and nourishing soups. There are also thick and wholesome soups made from puréed vegetables or meats. These are often ladled out as light meals in themselves.*

*The soups as served in India today are thus British in concept and Indian in content. They are generally water-based, whereas in the West soups are normally based on stocks. The first modern Indian soups were vegetarian – the sanitized version of mulligatawny taking the lead – and owe their origin to Southern India.*

# Mirchee Rasam

MULLIGATAWNY SOUP

Makes 900 ml/1½ pints/
4 cups

25 g/1 oz ghee
1 tablespoon mustard seeds
2 large onions, grated
2 cloves garlic, crushed
100 g/4 oz/¼ cup diced
mixed vegetables
pinch of asafoetida
1 tablespoon grated root
ginger
2 tablespoons saambhar
powder (see p.28)
2 tablespoons tomato purée
4 dry chillies, crushed
300 ml/½ pint/1¼ cups
vegetable ready gravy
(see p.35)
600 ml/1 pint/2½ cups
coconut milk
1 tablespoon salt, or to taste
1 teaspoon red chilli powder
6 tablespoons/½ cup
tamarind sauce
(see p.21)
25 g/1 oz/⅓ cup
desiccated coconut,
to garnish
lemon slices, to garnish

Prep 10 min
+ thawing time, if necessary
Cooking 20 min
+ standing time 5 min

*This distinguished offering from South India was created by the British and became the first official Indian vegetarian soup. Its name is derived from the Tamil words milagu and tunny or tannir, literally meaning 'chilli water'. Feel free to adapt the already moderated chilli content but, in any event, mind that skin on your tongue!*

1. Place the ghee in a lidded 3.6 litre/6 pint/15 cup casserole and microwave at full power for 2 minutes. Open the lid, add the mustard and cook, covered, on high for another 3 minutes, or until the seeds start spluttering.
2. Remove from the oven, add the rest of the ingredients except the coconut and lemon slices, and stir thoroughly. Cover and cook at full power for 12 minutes, stirring once or twice during cooking.
3. Remove the soup from the oven and let it stand for 5 minutes. Purée in a blender or food processor, then strain the soup and transfer it back to the casserole. Return to the oven and microwave on high for a further 3 minutes.
4. Ladle the soup into serving bowls and sprinkle with the desiccated coconut. Garnish each bowl with a twist of sliced lemon.

# Kaddu Rasam

## PUMPKIN SOUP

*A popular offering from the kitchens of Uttar Pradesh households, this attractive soup is light on the stomach and pleases the palate. An even lighter version is made from snake gourd (lauki). Serve hot or chilled.*

1. Place the pumpkin, tomato, potato and coconut milk in a 3.6 litre/6 pint/15 cups casserole and cook, covered, at full power for 5 minutes.
2. Leave the mixture to stand for 2 minutes then liquidize in a blender or food processor. Press the liquid through a sieve and transfer back to the casserole.
3. Add the water, lemon juice, salt and pepper and stir thoroughly. Return the soup to the oven and microwave at full power for 10 minutes, or until the soup is boiling. Stir a couple of times during cooking.
4. Remove the soup from the oven and serve immediately, sprinkled with the croûtons and coriander.

Makes 900 ml/1½ pints/
  4 cups

450 g/1 lb pumpkin, diced
1 large tomato, chopped
1 large potato, sliced
600 ml/1 pint/2½ cups
  coconut milk
300 ml/½ pint/1¼ cups
  water
1 tablespoon lemon juice
1½ teaspoons salt, or to
  taste
large pinch of freshly ground
  pepper
croûtons (see p.31), to
  garnish
2 tablespoons finely chopped
  coriander, to garnish

Prep 10 min
Cooking 15 min
+ standing time 2 min

# Moong aur Paalak Ka Shorwaa

SPINACH AND MUNG BEAN SOUP

Makes 600 ml/1 pint/2½ cups

1 tablespoon ghee
1 tablespoon finely chopped
  onion
100 g/4 oz/½ cup
  mung beans, soaked
225 g/8 oz/½ lb fresh
  spinach, chopped
2 teaspoons salt, or to taste
large pinch of black pepper
300 ml/½ pint/1¼ cups
  vegetarian ready gravy
  (see p.35)
300 ml/½ pint/1¼ cups water
1 tablespoon lemon juice
croûtons (see p.31), to
  garnish

Prep 15 min
+ soaking time
Cooking 20 min
+ standing time 2 min

*This light soup is a hot favourite of Popeye fans! It is rich in iron and nourishment and purifies the blood. Do adjust the thickness of the soup to your liking; cooking times may need to be adjusted accordingly.*

1. Place the ghee and onion in a 2.4 litre/4 pint/10 cup casserole and microwave on high for 2 minutes.
2. Add the mung beans, spinach, salt, pepper, ready gravy and water and cook, covered, at full power for 15 minutes, stirring a couple of times during cooking.
3. Remove the soup from the oven and leave it to stand for 2 minutes to complete the cooking process. Liquidize in a blender, add the lemon juice and return to the casserole. Cook at full power for 3 minutes.
4. Serve blazing hot, topping each serving with some croûtons.

# Shaahi Toor Rasam

TOOR (PIGEON PEAS) AND TOMATO SOUP

*Let us try to change the process of making the soup here: liquidize first and then cook. You can always choose which one, or a combination of these, you will use to garnish your soup: cream (single or double), herbs (coriander or mint), croûtons, freshly ground pepper, coarsely ground nuts (almonds, cashews, pistachios, walnuts) or lemon slices.*

1. Place the ghee or oil, mustard seeds, chillies, black pepper, asafoetida, onion and garlic in a microwavable casserole of 3.6 litre/6 pint/15 cup capacity. Cook, covered, at full power for 5 minutes.

2. Remove from the oven, add the rest of the ingredients, except the cream and coriander garnishes, and liquidize.

3. Transfer the soup back to the casserole, return to the oven and cook, covered, at full power for 10 minutes or until the soup is boiling. Stir once or twice during cooking. Leave to stand for 2 minutes to complete the cooking process.

4. Serve hot or cold, garnished with the cream and coriander, in that order.

Makes 900 ml/1½ pints/
 4 cups

2 tablespoons ghee or oil
1 tablespoon mustard seeds
2 whole dried chillies,
 crushed
1 teaspoon freshly ground
 black pepper
pinch of asafoetida powder
1 onion, finely sliced
2 cloves garlic, crushed
4 tablespoons toor daal,
 soaked
4 large tomatoes, chopped,
or 4 tablespoons tomato
 purée
2 green chillies, chopped
1 tablespoon grated root
 ginger
pinch of turmeric powder
600 ml/1 pint/2½ cups water
300 ml/½ pint/1¼ cups milk
1 tablespoon tamarind sauce
 (see p.21)
1 tablespoon salt, or to taste
4 tablespoons whipped
 cream, to garnish
4 tablespoons finely chopped
 coriander leaves, to garnish

Prep 15 min
+ soaking time
Cooking 15 min
+ standing time 2 min

# Baigan aur Podeena Rasam

## AUBERGINE AND MINT SOUP

Makes 900 ml/1½ pints/
 4 cups

1 large onion, chopped
1 tablespoon grated root
 ginger
2 cloves garlic, crushed
450 g/1 lb small aubergines/
 eggplants, chopped
2 small potatoes, diced
100 g/4 oz/½ cup
 lentils (masoor), soaked
300 ml/½ pint/1¼ cups milk
600 ml/1 pint/2½ cups water
4 tablespoons tomato purée
1 teaspoon red chilli powder
1 tablespoon salt, or to taste
4 tablespoons mint leaves,
 shredded, or 2 tablespoons
 dried mint
2 teaspoons freshly ground
 black pepper

Prep 10 min
+ soaking time
Cooking 15 min
+ standing time 2 min

*This fragrant, light and yet velvety soup can be enjoyed hot or chilled. If serving chilled, save half the mint to use as a garnish. Otherwise, ground pepper alone will be fine for the purpose.*

1. Place all the ingredients, excepting the ground pepper, in a microwave-friendly casserole of 3.6 litre/6 pint/15 cup capacity and cook at full power for 12 minutes, or until the vegetables and lentils are tender. Stir once or twice during cooking.
2. Remove the soup from the oven and leave it to stand for 2 minutes to complete the cooking process. Transfer the contents into a blender and liquidize to a coarsely textured purée.
3. Strain the soup and transfer it back to the casserole. Cook, covered, on high for another 3 minutes. Serve hot or chilled, sprinkled with ground pepper.

# Makkhani Gaajar Shorwaa

CREAMY CARROT SOUP

*'Soup of creamy carrots, crowned with croûtons', sounds aristocratic, doesn't it? Well, it is a sophisticated soup, quite capable of impressing the connoisseurs.*

1. Place the butter, onion, carrots, potato and orange zest in a casserole of 3.6 litre/6 pint/15 cup capacity and cook, covered, at full power for 5 minutes. Stir well.
2. Add the ready gravy, water, milk, salt and black pepper and cook, covered, at full power for 10 minutes, or until the vegetables are tender. Stir once during cooking.
3. Remove the soup from the oven and let it stand for 2 minutes. Liquidize, add the cream then return to the oven and microwave, covered, on high for a further 2 minutes.
4. Serve hot, crowned with croûtons.

Makes 900 ml/1½ pints/ 4 cups

50 g/2 oz/¼ cup unsalted butter
1 small onion, finely chopped
225 g/8 oz carrots, diced
1 small potato, sliced
grated zest of 1 orange
300 ml/½ pint/1¼ cups vegetarian ready gravy (see page 35)
600 ml/1 pint/2½ cups water
4 tablespoons/⅓ cup milk
2 teaspoons salt, or to taste
1 teaspoon freshly ground black pepper
4 tablespoons/⅓ cup whisked sour cream, to garnish
croûtons, to garnish

Prep 10 min
Cooking 17 min
+ standing time 2 min

# Sabziyon Ki Malaai Taree

CREAM OF VEGETABLE SOUP

Makes 600 ml/1 pint/2½ cups

2 large carrots, peeled
1 medium potato, peeled
4 spring onions
2 sticks celery
1 small cucumber
2 tablespoons tomato purée
300 ml/½ pint/1¼ cups milk
300 ml/½ pint/1¼ cups
    vegetarian ready gravy
    (see p.35)
salt and pepper
1 tablespoon lemon juice
whipped cream, to garnish

Prep 10 min
Cooking 20 min
+ standing time 2 min

*This is an excellent soup for young and old alike. Substitute fresh vegetables of your choice, or those in season, and delight your dinner guests. Serve hot or chilled.*

1. Chop all the vegetables roughly and place them in a 2.4 litre/4 pint/10 cup casserole together with the tomato purée, milk and gravy. Cover and cook at full power for 10 minutes.
2. Reduce the heat setting to medium and microwave for a further 8 minutes, or until the vegetables are tender.
3. Leave the soup to stand for 2 minutes to complete the cooking process, then liquidize and season to taste with salt and pepper. Stir in the lemon juice.
4. Reheat at full power for 2 more minutes then ladle the soup into individual bowls, topping each helping with a swirl of cream.

# Khumbi (Kukurmutta) aur Gaanthgobhi Rasam

MUSHROOM AND KOHLRABI BEELZEBUB

*This soup has novelty value for an Indian menu and, as its name suggests, is a bit on the fiery side. It repels cold and provides inner warmth. Feel free to adjust the flavourings to taste, particularly the chilli and pepper.*

1. In a suitable casserole of 3.6 litre/6 pint/15 cup capacity, cook the butter and cumin and microwave, uncovered, on high for 2 minutes.
2. Place the cornflour in a separate bowl and gradually stir in the milk and ready gravy. Blend thoroughly then add the mixture to the casserole.
3. Stir in the mushrooms, kohlrabi, tomato purée, salt, pepper and chilli powder and cook at full power for 10 minutes, or until the vegetables are tender and the soup is boiling. Stir once or twice during cooking and add the lemon juice 2 minutes before the end of the cooking time.
4. Remove the soup from the oven and leave to stand for 2 minutes, to complete the cooking process. Serve piping hot, topped with croûtons.

Makes 900 ml/1½ pints/4 cups

50 g/2 oz/¼ cup butter
1 tablespoon white cumin seeds
25 g/1 oz/¼ cup cornflour
300 ml/½ pint/1¼ cups milk
300 ml/½ pint/1¼ cups vegetarian ready gravy (see p.35)
100 g/4 oz/ ½ cup button mushrooms, thinly sliced
100 g/4oz/½ cup kohlrabi, thinly sliced
2 tablespoons tomato purée
salt, to taste
1 teaspoon ground black pepper
1 teaspoon red chilli powder
squeeze of lemon juice
croûtons, to garnish

Prep 10 min
Cooking 12 min
+ standing time 2 min

# Chaawal

## RICE

It is hard to imagine an Indian meal without rice, in one form or another. Rice is the staple food of millions of people in India, mainly in the south, in Bengal and Bihar.

In order to get the best results, buy the best quality rice. There are many varieties on the market, such as patna, basmataa (full of fragrance, male grain) and basmati (full of fragrance, female grain).

Most connoisseurs prefer basmati, a long-grained rice with a distinctive nutty fragrance. It has a unique cooking quality: unlike other varieties of rice, basmati increases in length when cooked, holds its shape and doesn't get mushy. The best prepared rice, when cooked, shows each grain separate, firm and fluffy, with no hard centre. I recommend the use of basmati in microwave ovens because the natural chemistry between this variety and the microwaves enables the grains to grow longer and fluffy, without breaking.

Conventionally, rice is pre-soaked and then cooked gently. In the microwave it cooks in two stages: first, uncovered boiling and second, covered steaming. This takes around 12 minutes and requires no pre-soaking. Although there is not much to gain in terms of cooking time, there are many other advantages to cooking rice in a microwave oven. It can be cooked exactly to the degree required and is almost impossible to burn or cook unevenly. Little attention is required during cooking in a microwave and your kitchen remains free of steam. In addition, the process of absorption (water soaking into the rice) retains all the vitamins and full flavour of the grain.

Cooked rice can be reheated successfully in the microwave. Basmati, like other starchy staples, loses its moisture content as it sits and tends to become dry so, before reheating, add a little butter to the cooked rice. Alternatively, rinse the cooked rice in cold water prior to reheating. The power level for reheating should be high or medium.

Frozen cooked rice can also be defrosted and reheated in your microwave. Add 15ml/1 tablespoon of water per 450 g/1 lb/2 cups of rice and defrost on low for 7 minutes, stirring halfway through with a fork. The rice can then be reheated on high or medium.

The dishes in this chapter range from plain preparations such as boiled rice, dalia and khichdee (all bland and light on the stomach) through steamed rice dishes from the south which are light, tasty and singularly ungreasy, to the plush pullaos and fascinating biriyanis enjoyed by the nobility.

Rice serves as the main antidote to India's spicy and hot dishes and thus exercises a generally moderating influence. It is worth noting, however, that pullaos and biriyanis are essentially gentle, mild dishes. Find your own level of 'mild' and then feel free to adjust the quantity of spices and other ingredients prescribed for those dishes.

People often ask me to define the main difference between pullaos and biriyanis. It is simple: pullaos, like other rice dishes in a meal, are served with another main dish like a curry; biriyanis, on the other hand, are a full meal in themselves, served only with ancillary side dishes such as a yoghurt preparation, poppadums, pickles and the like.

# Saada Ublaa Chaawal

BOILED RICE

*There is nothing to boiling rice in a microwave oven; it is quite straightforward. Use a glass bowl, casserole or a rice cooker of at least three times larger capacity than the quantity of rice. There is no need to soak the rice before cooking, nor is there need to stir during cooking, either. Serve with a daal or curry dish.*

Serves 4

225 g/8 oz/1 cup basmati rice
water, as required
pinch of salt
2 tablespoons ghee

Prep 10 min
Cooking 12 min
+ standing time 5 min

1. Pick over the rice as necessary, wash it in several changes of water then drain thoroughly.
2. Place the rice in a microwave-friendly bowl or dish of 1.8 litre/3 pint/7½ cup capacity. Add 600 ml/1 pint/2½ cups of cold water and the salt. Cook, uncovered, at full power for 8 minutes, or until the water has boiled and almost been absorbed by the rice.
3. Drain off the excess water then add the ghee to the rice and stir thoroughly with a fork. Cover and microwave on high for a further 4 minutes or until the moisture has evaporated and the surface of the rice has steam holes scattered across it.
4. Remove from the oven and let it stand, covered, for 5 minutes. Uncover, fluff up the rice with a fork and serve.

# Peelay Chaawal

## YELLOW RICE

Serves 4

225 g/8 oz/1 cup basmati rice
water, as required
1 teaspoon turmeric powder
pinch of salt
1 tablespoon ghee
2 tablespoons chopped
   coriander leaves

Prep 10 min
Cooking 12 min
+ standing time 5 min

*This preparation is often made by adding saffron strands – either on their own or steeped in a tablespoon of milk – in the second stage of cooking. However, this version is made with turmeric – a cheaper and more healthful alternative. It is more elegant to serve it with a non-vegetarian curry.*

1. Pick over the rice, wash it completely under a tap then drain thoroughly.
2. Place the rice in a glass bowl of 1.8 litre/3 pint/7½ cup capacity. Add 600ml/1 pint/2½ cups of water plus the turmeric and salt and cook, uncovered, at full power for 8 minutes, or until the water has come to a boil and begins to absorb into the rice.
3. Skim the surface of any scum and drain off the excess water. Add the ghee and stir well with a fork. Cover and cook at full power for a further 4 minutes, or until the moisture has evaporated and the surface of the rice has steam holes scattered across it.
4. Remove the rice from the oven and let it stand, covered, for 5 minutes. Uncover, fluff up the rice with a fork, fold in the coriander and serve.

# Chaawal Naariyal Paani

RICE IN COCONUT MILK

*The east, south-east, west and south-western
seaboards of India grow sumptuous quantities of
coconut so the food of these parts features it in
various forms. This particular preparation is ideally
made with fresh coconut milk. It brings balance to
a meal by countering the impact of hot chilli
concoctions made, for example, with fish – another
product of these regions.*

1. Pick over the rice, wash it completely under a tap then
drain thoroughly.
2. Place the rice in a suitable lidded glass bowl, or casserole
of 1.8 litre/3 pint/7½ cup capacity. Add the coconut milk and
stir well. Cook, uncovered, at full power for 10 minutes or
until the milk, after coming to the boil, has been absorbed by
the rice.
3. Drain off any excess milk, then cover and continue to cook
on high for a further 2 minutes.
4. Remove the rice from the oven and let it stand, covered,
for 5 minutes. Sprinkle the rice with the coconut and fluff up
with a fork before serving.

Serves 4

225 g/8 oz/1 cup basmati rice
600 ml/1 pint/2½ cups
   coconut milk
2 tablespoons desiccated
   coconut

Prep 5 min
Cooking 12 min
+ standing time 5 min

# Khichdee

BOILED RICE AND MUNG BEANS

Serves 4

100 g/4 oz/½ cup mung beans
100 g/4 oz/½ cup basmati rice
600 ml/1 pint/2½ cups water
½ teaspoon turmeric powder
1 teaspoon salt, or to taste
50 g/2 oz/¼ cup ghee
1 teaspoon white cumin
  seeds (optional)
pinch of asafoetida powder
  (optional)
1 green chilli, chopped
  (optional)

Prep 10 min
+ soaking time
Cooking 12 min
+ standing time 5 min

*Instead of cooking rice and daal separately, why not cook the two together. Khichdee, by tradition, is made with mung beans and is light on the stomach. You can also make it with black beans (urad). My mother's dictum about this dish is: 'Khichdee ke chaar yaar: dahi, paapad, ghee, achaar.' (Khichdee has four lovers: yoghurt, poppadums, clarified butter and pickles.)*

1. Soak the beans for 30 minutes in warm water then wash thoroughly, draining off the water completely.
2. Pick over the rice, wash it thoroughly under a tap then drain thoroughly.
3. Place the measured water in a microwave-safe casserole of 1.8 litre/3 pint/7½ cup capacity. Add the rice, beans, turmeric and salt and cook, uncovered, on full power for 10 minutes, or until the water has been absorbed into the rice and the beans are tender.
4. Stir once, add the ghee, then cover and cook at full power for a further 2 minutes. Leave to stand, covered, for 5 minutes.
5. Fluff up the mixture with a fork and serve hot, with any or all of the remaining 3 ingredients.

Variations: if desired, caramelized onions (see p.32), sautéed cumin (see p.33) or glazed mustard (see p.34) can be heated and added to the khichdee before serving.

# Saada Dalia

FUNDAMENTAL RICE

*This moist porridge-like dish is a light meal or one for when your stomach feels delicate. It can also be served with milk as a breakfast cereal. An alternative dish could be made from coarsely ground wheat grains. In the microwave, it cooks like a dream: a creamy texture, without lumps, every time! Adjust the cooking times to give a dalia of your preferred thickness.*

Serves 4

175 g/6 oz coarsely ground
rice
600 ml/1 pint/2½ cups water

Prep 5 min
Cooking 10 min
+ standing time 5 min

1. In a microwave-safe casserole of 2.4 litre/4 pint/10 cup capacity, combine the ground rice and water and cook, uncovered, at full power for 8 minutes, or until the water comes to a boil. Stop and stir soon after the mixture has boiled.
2. Remove the casserole from the oven, stir once or twice then cover and cook on high for another 2 minutes.
3. Let the mixture stand, covered, for 5 minutes. Serve either as a cereal with milk and sugar; or as a meal, sprinkled with lemon juice, salt and pepper and accompanied by ready gravy and/or salad.

# Idlee

## STEAMED RICE CAKES

Serves 4

100 g/4 oz/1 cup ground rice
50 g/2 oz/½ cup black bean
 (urad daal) flour
½ teaspoon bicarbonate of
 soda
½ teaspoon salt
water, as necessary
oil, for greasing

Prep 10 min
+ fermenting time
Cooking 4 min
+ standing time 2 min

*This popular south Indian dish from the Madras region cooks beautifully in a microwave oven – no elaborate steaming paraphernalia is required. These savoury cakes are very light and can be served as a small meal or with afternoon tea, with any south Indian chutney or curry of your choice. Leftover idlees can be toasted, with a filling if desired, in a normal sandwich toaster. Alternatively, they can be turned into a different type of snack: chop up the idlees, spice them and deep-fry on a conventional cooker. A similar dish, made from a batter of black or mung bean powder, with a little rice flour, is made in the Gujerat region and is called dhokla (lentil cakes).*

1. In a large bowl of 1.8 litre/3 pint/7½ cup capacity, combine the rice, black bean flour, soda and salt and, with the help of some water, make a batter of dropping consistency. Leave the bowl, uncovered, in a warm place overnight; the batter will swell up to double its original volume by morning.
2. Lightly grease a 12-hole egg-poacher (or cook two batches in a smaller size). Pour the batter into each depression, filling it halfway up the sides.
3. Cook, uncovered, at full power for 4 minutes (or for 2 minutes if using a smaller poacher), or until the idlees have risen. To test for doneness, insert a cocktail stick in the middle of an idlee and, if it comes out clean, the idlees are ready.
4. Remove the idlees from the moulds using a sharp knife. Leave to stand for 2 minutes before serving with coconut chutney (see page 170) or saambhar (see page 180).

# Chaawal Upmaa

## BEATEN RICE MISHMASH

*Upmaa is a southern Indian rice mishmash. It can also be made with wheat or other cereals. The moist heat of the microwave is ideal for cooking this dish: when the grains absorb the moisture, they become soft and plump and taste something like pasta! Eager mouths receive this luscious upmaa with gratitude at any time of the day – breakfast, lunch or afternoon tea.*

1. Spread the coarsely ground rice on an ungreased microwave-proof dinner plate and roast it, uncovered, at full power for 2 minutes, stirring halfway through cooking.
2. Heat the ghee in a covered casserole at full power for 1 minute. Add the mustard seeds, replace the lid and cook, covered, at full power for 2 minutes, or until the mustard seeds begin to splutter.
3. Stir in the asafoetida, vegetables, salt, green chillies and legume powder, mixing well. Cook, uncovered, on high for another 3 minutes, or until the vegetables look glazed. Stir once during cooking.
4. Pour in the measured water and roasted rice and cook, uncovered, at full power for 4 minutes, stirring halfway through. The rice particles should look cooked and puffy.
5. Cover with the lid and cook at full power for another 3 minutes, or until the mixture is almost dry and the water is completely absorbed.
6. Remove the casserole from the oven, add the lemon juice and blend well. Scatter the green coriander over the mixture, cover with the lid and let it stand for 5 minutes.
7. Fluff the rice up with a fork and either serve the mixture as it is, or shape it into small balls or discs and serve hot with a sauce such as saambhar (see p.180) or coconut chutney (see p.170).

Serves 4

100 g/4 oz/1 cup
   coarsely ground rice
1 tablespoon ghee
1 teaspoon mustard seeds
pinch of asafoetida powder
175 g/6 oz/1 cup diced mixed
   vegetables, such as
   carrots, onion, peas, green
   pepper and potatoes
1 teaspoon salt, or to taste
2 green chillies, chopped
1 tablespoon mixed legume
   (daal) powder
300 ml/½ pint/1¼ cups
   lukewarm water
1 teaspoon lemon juice
2 tablespoons chopped
   coriander leaves

Prep 10 min
Cooking 15 min
+ standing time 5 min

# Chaawal Pottu

## COCONUT RICE CAKES

Serves 4

300 ml/½ pint/1¼ cups
  coconut milk
100 g/4 oz/1 cup ground rice
½ teaspoon bicarbonate of
  soda
½ teaspoon salt
2 large egg whites
oil, for greasing

Prep 10 min
+ fermenting time
Cooking 4 min
+ standing time 2 min

*This dish is a Tamil speciality, inspired by Sri Lankan cuisine. The inclusion of coconut milk accentuates the sweet and aromatic taste while the egg-whisk renders the cakes feather-light! Usually served with spicy (and hot) curried dishes, mainly fish, but do feel free to experiment with alternatives.*

1. In a large bowl of 1.8 litre/3 pint/7½ cup capacity, combine the coconut milk, rice, soda and salt and whisk into a batter of dropping consistency. Leave the bowl, uncovered, in a warm place overnight; the batter will have risen to double its original volume by the morning.
2. Beat the egg whites in a separate bowl until stiff then fold into the risen rice batter.
3. Lightly grease the depressions of a 12-egg poaching tray (or cook in two batches using a 6-egg-poacher). Pour the batter into each depression, filling it halfway up.
4. Cook, uncovered, at full power for 4 minutes (reduce the time to 2 minutes if using the smaller poacher), or until the pottus have risen. To test for doneness, insert a cocktail stick in the middle of a pottu and, if it comes out clean, the cakes are ready.
5. Remove the cakes from the moulds using a sharp knife. Cover and leave to stand for 2 minutes before serving with a fish dish and sauces or chutneys of your choice.

# Tiranga Sabzi Pullao

TRICOLOUR VEGETARIAN PULLAO

*This is a basic vegetarian pullao that can be served with all kinds of curries. Adapt the quantity and variety of vegetables to your liking. If preferred, collect all the colours of the rainbow in vegetables and call it a rainbow pullao!*

1. Wash and soak the rice in warm water for 10 minutes. In a separate pan, covered with a lid, soak the vegetables in hot water for 10 minutes. Drain off the water and keep the rice and vegetables separate.

2. In a microwave-friendly casserole of 1.8 litre/3 pint/7½ cup capacity, place the ghee and onion and microwave on high for 3 minutes, stirring once during cooking. Remove from the oven and reserve half the onion for later use.

3. To the remaining ghee and onion in the bowl, add the cumin seeds, turmeric, tomato and cardamom, stir a few times then cook at full power for another 2 minutes.

4. Stir in the vegetables and rice, then pour in the water and add a little salt. Cook, uncovered, at full power for 9 minutes, or until the water has boiled and soaked into the rice.

5. Drain off any excess water, then stir the mixture with a fork, sprinkle with the garam masala, and cover with the lid. Return to the microwave and cook at full power for 4 minutes.

6. Leave the pullao to stand, covered, for 5 minutes. Uncover, fluff up the rice with a fork, scatter over the reserved onion and serve garnished with foil.

Serves 4

225 g/8 oz/1 cup basmati rice
225 g/8 oz/½ cup diced mixed vegetables of 3 prominent colours, such as carrots, peas and potatoes
50 g/2 oz/¼ cup ghee
2 small onions, chopped
½ teaspoon white cumin seeds
½ teaspoon turmeric powder
1 large tomato, chopped
½ teaspoon seeds from green cardamom pods
600 ml/1 pint/2½ cups water
salt and pepper, to taste
2 teaspoons garam masala
edible silver foils, to garnish

Prep 10 min
+ soaking time
Cooking 18 min
+ standing time 5 min

# Baigan aur Guchhi Ka Pullao
AUBERGINE AND MUSHROOM PULLAO

**Serves 4**

1 small aubergine, weighing
  about 100 g/4 oz
100 g/4 oz/1 cup mushrooms
water, as required
2 tablespoons ghee
1 tablespoon chopped onion
1 teaspoon white cumin
  seeds
pinch of asafoetida powder
225 g/8 oz/1 cup basmati rice
salt, to taste
½ teaspoon red chilli
  powder
slices of lemon and green
  pepper, to garnish

**Prep 10 min**
**Cooking 20 min**
**+ standing time 5 min**

*This delightful dish should be an instant hit at your dinner table. In order to achieve and enhance the authentic flavour, try and use fresh or tinned black mushrooms (guchhi), obtainable from selected Asian grocers.*

1. Clean, wash and chop the aubergine and mushrooms. Place in a microwave-safe casserole of 1.8 litre/3 pint/7½ cup capacity, add water to cover and cook, uncovered, at full power for 4 minutes. Remove from the oven, drain off the water, transfer the vegetables to a plate and reserve.
2. Place the ghee in the same casserole and cook, uncovered, at full power for 1 minute. Add the onion and cook at full power for 3 minutes. Stir in the cumin and asafoetida until thoroughly combined.
3. Add 600 ml/1 pint/2½ cups of water to the casserole, stir in the rice, salt, chilli powder and parboiled vegetables and cook on high for 8 minutes, or until the water boils and is absorbed by the rice.
4. Drain off any excess water, then stir the mixture with a fork, taking care not to mash the vegetables. Cover and cook at full power for another 4 minutes, or until the moisture has evaporated and each grain of rice is separate.
5. Remove the pullao from the oven and leave it, covered, to stand for 5 minutes. Carefully fluff up the rice with a fork and serve garnished with the slices of lemon and green pepper. Eat with any of the curries and/or one or more of the usual rice accompaniments – yoghurt preparation, poppadum and pickles.

# Swaadisht Murghi Pullao

FINGER LICKIN' CHICKEN RICE

*This preparation will serve four people generously. Feel free to adjust the quantities of chicken and spices to your liking. A similar pullao can be made with lamb.*

1. Pierce the chicken pieces all over with a fork. Smear thickly with the yoghurt and leave to marinade for at least 30 minutes. Meanwhile, wash and soak the rice in warm water for 10 minutes. After marinading and soaking, rinse both the chicken and rice and drain thoroughly.
2. Place the chicken in a microwavable casserole of 2.4 litre/4 pint/10 cup capacity. Add sufficient water to come 1 cm/½ inch above the chicken. On a clean piece of muslin or other thin cloth, put a pinch each of salt, asafoetida and black cumin plus the garam masala, cloves, brown cardamom and bay leaves. Tie into a loose bag and drop it into the casserole. Cook uncovered on high for 6 minutes, or until the chicken pieces change colour and become tender.
3. Drain the cooking water into a measuring jug and add sufficient fresh water to bring the total liquid to 600 ml/ 1 pint/2½ cups. Stir the water and rice back into the casserole with additional salt to taste, the chilli powder and the green cardamoms. Cook, uncovered, at full power for 8 minutes, or until the water has boiled and soaked into the pullao.
4. Drain off any excess liquid, then stir the pullao with a fork, cover with a lid and cook on high for another 4 minutes.
5. Remove the pullao from the oven and discard the spice bag. Sprinkle the caramelized onion over the pullao, cover and leave to stand for 5 minutes. Fluff up the pullao with a fork and serve hot with the desired accompaniments.

Serves 4

450 g/1 lb small meaty chicken pieces
plain yoghurt, for marinading
450 g/1 lb/2 cups basmati rice
water, as required
salt, to taste
pinch of asafoetida powder
large pinch of black cumin seeds
1 teaspoon garam masala
4 cloves
1 brown cardamom pod, cracked
2 bay leaves
1 teaspoon red chilli powder
4 green cardamom pods, cracked
4 tablespoons ghee
2 tablespoons caramelized onions (see p.32)

Prep 15 min
+ marinading and soaking times
Cooking 18 min
+ standing time 5 min

# Jheenga Kathak Pullao

PRAWN AND RICE PULLAO

Serves 4

225 g/8 oz/1 cup basmati rice
water, as required
50 g/2 oz/¼ cup unsalted
   butter
100 g/4 oz/1 cup spring
   onions, chopped
300 ml/½ pint/1¼ cups
   prawns, peeled
75 g/3 oz/½ cup green peas
1 tablespoon tomato purée
salt and ground pepper, to
   taste
2 fresh firm tomatoes, sliced,
   to garnish

Prep 10 min
Cooking 13 min
+ standing time 5 min

*This is an elegant piscatorial delight which fish-lovers – Bengalis in particular – love to offer their guests. Whenever you cook it, its fragrant memory will haunt you a good while longer!*

1. Pick over the rice, wash it in several changes of water then drain thoroughly.

2. Place the rice and 300ml/½ pint/1¼ cups of water in a microwave-safe casserole of 2.4 litre/4 pint/10 cup capacity. Cook, uncovered, at full power for 4 minutes. Drain and transfer the rice to a separate dish.

3. Place the butter, onions and prawns in the casserole and stir to combine. Cook, uncovered, at full power for 4 minutes.

4. Add the rice, peas, tomato purée and seasoning to the casserole plus 150ml/¼ pint/⅔ cup of fresh water. Cover and microwave on high for another 5 minutes, or until the liquid has been fully absorbed into the pullao.

5. Remove from the oven and leave to stand, covered, for 5 minutes. Fluff up the pullao with a fork and serve hot, garnished with the tomato slices.

# Sapnaa Gobhi Biriyaani

CAULIFLOWER DREAM BIRIYANI

*A biriyani without meat is something special – simple and yet so delicious. This particular dish is for the connoisseur: impress and delight your dinner guests with your biriyani-making prowess. They will dream about it for a long time!*

1. Mix the rice with the ready gravy in a microwave-safe casserole of 1.8 litre/3 pint/7½ cup capacity and cook, uncovered, at full power for 5 minutes. Remove from the oven, cover and set aside.
2. In another casserole, place the cauliflower and sufficient water to submerge the florets and cook, uncovered, at full power for 5 minutes. Remove from the oven, drain, cover and set aside.
3. Take another casserole of 1.8 litre/3 pint/7½ cup capacity, and add the ghee, cumin seeds, asafoetida, bay leaves, turmeric and cloves and cook, uncovered, at full power for 2 minutes. Stir in the tomato purée, yoghurt and green cardamom and
continue cooking on full power for another 3 minutes.
4. Add the rice and its cooking liquid, plus the drained cauliflower to the casserole. Stir in salt and pepper to taste and cook, uncovered, on high for 5 minutes, or until the liquid has been absorbed by the rice.
5. Sprinkle the biriyani with garam masala, cover and cook on high for a further 2 minutes. Remove from the oven and leave to stand, covered, for 5 minutes.
6. Fluff up the rice with a fork and serve hot, garnishing each individual portion with a piece of edible foil.

Serves 4

225 g/8 oz/1 cup basmati rice
300 ml/½ pint/1¼ cups vegetarian ready gravy (see p.35)
225 g/8 oz/2 cups cauliflower florets
water, as required
4 tablespoons ghee
2 teaspoons white cumin seeds
pinch of asafoetida powder
2 bay leaves
½ teaspoon turmeric powder
4 cloves
2 tablespoons tomato purée
4 tablespoons plain yoghurt
4 green cardamom pods, cracked
salt, to taste
freshly ground black pepper
1 teaspoon garam masala
gold or silver edible foils, to garnish

Prep 10 min
Cooking 22 min
+ standing time 5 min

# Anday Ki Biriyaani

### EGG BIRIYANI

Serves 4

8 large eggs
450 g/1 lb/2 cups basmati rice
6 tablespoons/½ cup ghee
1 large onion, finely chopped
2 cloves garlic, crushed
2 bay leaves
2 cinnamon sticks, each
   about 2.5 cm/1inch long
1 brown cardamom pod,
   cracked
½ teaspoon turmeric powder
1 teaspoon red chilli powder
4 green cardamom pods,
   cracked
600 ml/1 pint/2½ cups meat
   or chicken ready gravy
   (see p.36)
salt, to taste
50 g/2 oz/½ cup flaked
   almonds and cashews
50 g/2 oz/⅓ cup sultanas
2 tablespoons drained
   caramelized onions
   (see p.32)

Prep 20 min
+ soaking time
Cooking 22 min
+ standing time 5 min

*This concoction is something of a bridge between the vegetarian and non-vegetarian dishes of India. Feel free to experiment with alternative ingredients.*

1. Hard-boil the eggs at full power in a microwave-compatible egg boiler – this takes, on average, 2 minutes per egg. Leave to cool then peel the eggs. Using a cocktail stick, pierce the eggs all over, without breaking them. (This step can be done in advance and the eggs put in a covered container in the refrigerator.)
2. Pick over the rice, wash it thoroughly then soak it in warm water for 10 minutes. Drain off the water and set the rice aside on a plate or in a bowl.
3. Meanwhile, in a microwavable casserole of 2.4 litre/4 pint/10 cup capacity, mix 4 tablespoons of the ghee with the onion and garlic and cook, uncovered, on high for 3 minutes. Stir in the bay leaves, cinnamon sticks, brown cardamom pod, turmeric and chilli powder and continue cooking for another 2 minutes, stirring once halfway through.
4. Add the whole hard-boiled eggs and green cardamom pods to the mixture and stir carefully to blend. Add the rice and mix. Cook, uncovered, at full power for a further 2 minutes.
5. Pour the gravy into the casserole, add salt to taste and cook, uncovered, at full power for 8 minutes, or until the gravy has boiled and been absorbed into the rice. Remove from the oven and stir with a fork.
6. In a microwavable skillet, heat the remaining 2 tablespoons of ghee at full power for 1 minute. Add the almonds, cashews and sultanas and cook for 2 minutes, or until the nuts are browned and the sultanas begin to swell (with pride!).
7. Scatter the nut and fruit mixture over the biriyani, cover with the lid and cook at full power for 4 minutes. Remove from the oven, add the garam masala and caramelized onion and leave to stand, covered, for 5 minutes. Fluff up the rice with a fork before serving the dish hot.

# Nawaabi Kofta Biriyaani

## PRINCELY MEATBALLS BIRIYANI

*This is the objet d'art of the biriyani world! It is a substantial dish and was very popular with the Mughal nobility at Delhi, Agra and Oudh. Why not elevate the environment of your dining room by offering this princely fare to your near and dear ones?*

1. Pick over the rice and soak it in warm water for 15-20 minutes. Meanwhile, prepare the garnish of nuts and fruit. In a microwavable skillet, heat 2 tablespoons of ghee at full power for 1 minute. Add the almonds, cashews and sultanas and cook for 2 minutes, or until the nuts are browned and the sultanas begin to swell. Remove from the oven and set aside. When the rice has finished soaking, drain it thoroughly and set aside.

2. In a large bowl, mix the lamb, garam masala, mango powder, coconut, garlic and ginger together with a large pinch of salt. Add the egg and blend in well. Divide the mixture into 16 portions and shape into small balls.

3. Place the measured water in a microwave-proof casserole of 1.8 litre/3 pint/7$^1$/$_2$ cup capacity. Heat, uncovered, at full power for 8 minutes or until the water comes to a rolling boil. Remove the dish from the oven and carefully drop in the meatballs. Return to the oven and cook, uncovered, at full power for 5 minutes. Take out the meatballs and set them aside on a plate while at the same time reserving the liquid, covered, for later use.

4. To make the spice cooking mixture, place the ghee in a microwave-safe casserole of 2.4 litre/4 pint/10 cup capacity and cook, uncovered, at full power for 1 minute. Add the asafoetida, cumin seeds, chilli powder, bay leaves, cardamom pods and cinnamon and continue to cook, uncovered, at full power for another 2 minutes, or until the spices exude their aroma. Stop and stir once during cooking.

5. Remove the spice mixture from the oven, add the meatballs and blend carefully. Tip the drained rice over the top, pour in the reserved liquid and then the ready stock. Cover and cook at full power for 8 minutes.

**Serves 4**

450 g/1 lb/2 cups basmati rice
450 g/1 lb lean lamb, finely minced
1 teaspoon garam masala
½ teaspoon mango powder (aamchur)
1 tablespoon desiccated coconut
1 clove garlic, crushed
1 teaspoon grated root ginger
salt, to taste
1 medium egg
600 ml/1 pint/2½ cups lukewarm water
300 ml/½ pint/1¼ cups meat ready gravy (see p.36)
1 teaspoon saffron strands
2 tablespoons rose water

For the spice mixture:
2 tablespoons ghee
pinch of asafoetida powder
½ teaspoon black cumin seeds, or 1 teaspoon white cumin seeds
1 teaspoon red chilli powder
2 bay leaves
4 green cardamom pods, cracked
2 cinnamon sticks, about 2.5 cm/1 inch, broken

(continued overleaf)

For the garnish:
2 tablespoons ghee
50 g/2 oz mixed flaked
   almonds and cashews
50g/2oz sultanas
caramelized onions
   (see p.32), optional
edible foils

Prep 15 min
+ soaking time
Cooking 30 min
+ standing time 5 min

6. Meanwhile, steep the saffron in the rose water and sprinkle the mixture over the biriyani at the end of the cooking period. Stir carefully with a fork and add the garnishes. Cover the casserole with the lid and cook on high for another 2 minutes, or until the liquid has been absorbed and the excess has evaporated.

7. Take the casserole out of the oven and leave, covered, to stand for 5 minutes. Fluff up the rice with a fork, being careful not to break up the meatballs, and serve, topping each portion with a piece of foil.

# Rotiyaan

BREADS

*Indian breads are well known throughout the world and are in a class by themselves. They can be made from the flours of corn and other grains, greens such as methi, and even of fruits, for example water chestnuts. While it is true that most Indian breads cannot be eaten by themselves, it is also true that most Indian meals are not considered complete without a bread dish.*

*Unfortunately, it is not possible to deep-fry food in a microwave oven and, as a consequence, very many types of breads have had to be excluded from this section. For the breads that are included, there is still the problem of browning. Breads can be browned in your microwave if it has a built-in browning facility. Alternatively, you can use a browning skillet, or cook the breads in the microwave and then smear them with a mixture of ghee and chilli powder, or paprika or tandoori powder.*

# Chapatty
## BASIC BREAD

Serves 4

450 g/1 lb/4 cups wholemeal
  flour
pinch of salt
water, as necessary
oil, for greasing
ghee (optional)
pinch of red chilli powder
  (optional)

Prep 10 min
+ resting time
Cooking 12 min

*Chapatty is an essential component of an Indian meal. It is usually served with a lentil or curry dish.*

1. Set aside a little of the flour for dredging, then place the remainder in a deep bowl with the salt. Add just enough water to give a soft, pliable dough. Knead lightly then leave the dough to rest for 30 minutes, covered with a damp cloth.
2. Knead the dough again and divide it into 12 portions, rolling each of them into a ball. Dredge each ball generously with the reserved flour. Flatten each ball a little and roll it into a thin, round disc using a board and rolling pin (chakla-belan).
3. Wipe the surface of a microwave-safe shallow dish or browning skillet with oil and place one of the discs on it. Cook, uncovered, at full power for 30 seconds on each side. Repeat with the remaining discs. Then, either brown each chapatty under a hot conventional grill, or smear the top with a mixture of ghee and chilli powder before serving.

# Makke di Roti

## CORNFLOUR BREAD

*A typical cornflour bread is thick and large (similar to those made from millet or water-chestnut flours), and should be served with a lot of ghee spread over the surface. These breads go well with a daal or curry.*

1. Sift the cornflour into a basin. Gradually add enough cold milk to make a pliable dough. Knead the dough for about 5 minutes then leave to rest, covered with a damp cloth, for some 20 minutes.
2. Knead the dough again for a further 5 minutes and divide it into eight portions. Using damp hands, flatten each portion into round discs. Any discs not in use should be covered with a damp cloth.
3. Wipe the surface of a microwave-safe shallow dish or browning skillet with oil and place one of the rounds on it. Cook, uncovered, on high for 1 minute on each side then repeat with the remaining rounds.
4. You may brown each bread under a conventional grill for a few seconds, or mix together some ghee and chilli powder and smear the paste on the surface of each bread to impart a cooked appearance.

Serves 4

450 g/1 lb/4 cups cornflour
milk, as necessary
oil, for greasing
ghee (optional)
pinch of red chilli powder
 (optional)

**Prep 12 min
+ resting time
Cooking 16 min**

# Methi Tikki

## FENUGREEK BREAD

Serves 4

225 g/8 oz/1 cup fenugreek
leaves, (methi ka saag)
225 g/8 oz/2 cups gram flour
(besan)
pinch of salt
pinch of carom seeds
(ajwaain)
pinch of garam masala
water, as necessary
plain flour, for dredging
oil, for greasing
ghee (optional)
large pinch of red chilli
powder (optional)

Prep 15 min
+ resting time
Cooking 12 min

*This is a wholesome and delicious variety of bread, but it can be heavy on the stomach. Those with frail digestive systems should eat this bread only sparingly.*

1. Clean and grind the fenugreek then place it in a deep mixing bowl. Stir in the flour, salt, carom seeds and garam masala. Add just enough water to make a medium-soft yet pliable dough then leave it to rest for 30 minutes.
2. Knead the dough lightly then divide it into eight portions. Shape them into balls. Dredge each one generously with plain flour and roll it into a thin, round disc. Once all the balls have been rolled into discs, cover then with a damp cloth.
3. Wipe the base of a microwave-friendly shallow dish or browning skillet with oil and place one disc on it. Cook, uncovered, at full power for 45 seconds on each side then repeat with the remaining discs.
4. Mix the ghee and chilli powder together and smear the mixture generously on the surface of each roti, as it comes out of the oven. Serve hot, one by one.

# Bharwaan Roti

## STUFFED BREAD

*Those with healthy appetites and strong digestive systems will love this bread, especially after a hard morning's work. Serve accompanied by a substantial daal dish such as Pulses and Marrow (p.102) or Plump Black-eyed Peas (p.100).*

1. Place the wholemeal flour in a mixing bowl. Make a well in the middle and add sufficient water to knead into a medium-soft dough. Divide the mixture into eight portions and, using lightly greased hands, form each into a small, round disc. Leave to rest while you make the stuffing.
2. In another bowl, place the black-bean powder, asafoetida, garam masala, garlic and salt. Add enough water to bind the ingredients into a smooth stuffing then divide the mixture into eight portions.
3. Take one disc of dough, place a portion of stuffing on it and roll it up into a ball, enveloping the stuffing. Repeat with the remaining dough and stuffing.
4. Generously dredge each ball with plain flour and roll it out into a thinnish round disc. The discs not being used should be covered with a damp cloth.
5. Wipe the base of a microwave-safe shallow dish or a browning skillet with oil and place a bread disc on it. Cook, uncovered, at full power for 45 seconds on each side. Similarly cook the other discs.
6. Mix the ghee with the tandoori masala and smear this mixture generously on the top of each roti when it is cooked. Serve hot, straight from the oven.

Serves 4

225 g/8 oz/2 cups wholemeal flour
water, as required
100 g/4 oz/1 cup black-bean (urad) powder
pinch of asafoetida powder
½ teaspoon garam masala
2 cloves garlic, crushed
½ teaspoon salt, or to taste
plain flour, for dredging
oil, for greasing
ghee (optional)
½ teaspoon tandoori masala (see p.29)

Prep 15 min
+ resting time
Cooking 12 min

# Naan

## LEAVENED BAKED BREAD

Serves 4

225 g/8 oz/2 cups plain flour
1 teaspoon sugar
1 teaspoon salt, or to taste
½ teaspoon bicarbonate of
  soda
1 teaspoon fresh yeast
150 ml/¼ pint/⅔ cup warm
  milk
150 ml/¼ pint/⅔ cup natural
  yoghurt
oil, for greasing
100 g/4 oz/½ cup butter
2-3 tablespoons poppy seeds

Prep 30 min
+ rising time
Cooking 14 min

*This dish is an offering from the Punjab region of India. It goes well with tandoori meat dishes or hot, tangy vindaloos. Traditionally, this bread is cooked in a tandoor (clay oven); you may, however, show off your culinary dexterity by cooking it in a microwave.*

1. Sift the flour into a large bowl then stir in the sugar, salt and soda. Dissolve the yeast in the milk and stir in the yoghurt. Add this mixture to the flour and blend thoroughly to form a dough. Knead for about 20 minutes until smooth then cover and leave to rise in a warm place for about 4 hours.
2. Divide the risen dough into eight equal portions and roll them into balls. On a lightly floured surface, flatten the balls a little then shape them into oblongs by slapping the naan from one hand to the other.
3. Wipe the surface of a microwave-proof shallow dish or a browning skillet with oil and place one naan on it. Microwave on high for 1 minute 30 seconds. Spread the raw side of the bread with butter and poppy seeds.
4. If your microwave does not have an in-built browning facility and you are not using a browning skillet, transfer the naan to a conventional hot grill for browning – this should take just a few seconds. Cook the other naans similarly and serve hot, one by one, as they are cooked.

# Moong Ka Chilla

MUNG BEAN PANCAKE

*Chillas are similar to pancakes or crêpes but in India, chillas are regarded as bread. This one is light on the stomach and can be made savoury or sweet. Chillas are usually made from daal (bean) flour, rice flour or gram flour (besan). Serve with caviar, or a preferred yoghurt dish, chutney or pickle preparation.*

1. Place the flour in a mixing bowl and gradually stir in just enough water to make a thin batter of dropping consistency. Stir in the salt, chillies, garam masala and coriander and mix well. Leave to rest for 5 minutes.
2. Take a microwave-compatible shallow dish or a browning skillet and brush its base with 1 teaspoon of oil. Cover with a lid and heat at full power for 2 minutes. Remove from the oven, uncover and drop 2 tablespoons of batter on to the dish, spreading it out evenly to the desired thickness (bean batters do not flow, they have to be coaxed). Baste the pancake with another ½ teaspoon of oil then turn it over, return to the microwave and cook, uncovered, at full power for 30 seconds.
3. With the remaining batter, make three more chillas in the same fashion, cooking each one for 45 seconds on each side at full power. Baste both sides of the chilla with a little oil.
4. Chillas can assume a brown look when cooked in a microwave with built-in browning facility, or in a browning skillet. Otherwise, place under a hot conventional grill for 10 seconds on each side then serve hot.

**Serves 4**

225 g/8 oz/2 cups dried mung
   bean flour
water, as required
salt, to taste
2 green chillies, chopped
pinch of garam masala
1 tablespoon coriander
   leaves, shredded
oil, for greasing

**Prep 10 min**
**+ resting time**
**Cooking 7 min**

# Andaa-Maida Chilla

## EGG-FLOUR PANCAKE

**Serves 4**

100 g/4 oz/1 cup plain flour
salt, to taste
2 eggs
300 ml/½ pint/1¼ cups milk
pinch of freshly ground black
   pepper
oil, for greasing

Prep 10 min
+ rising
Cooking 17 min
+ standing time 5 min

*Like other chillas, this one is also regarded as bread. When ready, you can place 1 tablespoon of a ready-cooked vegetarian or non-vegetarian dry dish on the chilla and wrap it up from both sides, rather like a masala dosa. Serve with a yoghurt preparation or saambhar sauce (see p.180).*

1. Sift the flour and a pinch of salt into a large bowl. In a separate bowl, crack and beat the eggs, pour in the milk and add the black pepper. Transfer this mixture, slowly, to the flour together with any additional salt required. Beat thoroughly to give a smooth batter then leave to stand for 5 minutes.

2. Take a microwave-proof shallow dish or a browning skillet and brush its base with 1 teaspoon of oil. Heat it, covered, at full power for 2 minutes. Remove from the oven and pour 2 tablespoons of batter on to the base, spreading it out evenly.
Brush another ½ teaspoon of oil on top then turn over and return to the microwave. Cook, uncovered, at full power for 1 minute. Remove the chilla with a wooden spatula and brown under a conventional grill, if desired.

3. With the remaining batter, make seven more chillas, basting them with a little oil and cooking at full power for 1 minute on each side.

# Saada Dosa

## PLAIN DOSA

*Plain dosa can be described as a rice 'chilla'. It is a south Indian dish which can be served plain, or with stuffing (either vegetarian or non-vegetarian – see egg-flour pancake recipe p.90). The side dishes that inevitably accompany the dosa are coconut chutney (p.170) and saambhar (p.180); or a sour or sweet-and-sour chutney with a non-vegetarian filling.*

1. Mix the urad and rice flours together with the soda in a deep bowl. Add sufficient water to make a frothy batter of pouring consistency. Stir in the salt and mix thoroughly. Leave to stand for 15 minutes.
2. Take a microwave-friendly shallow dish or browning skillet and brush its base with 1 teaspoon of oil. Cover with a lid and heat at full power for 2 minutes. Remove from the oven, lift the lid and carefully drop 2 tablespoons of batter on to the surface, spreading it out evenly. Apply another ½ teaspoon of oil to the top of the dosa then turn it over, return to the microwave and cook, uncovered, on high for 1 minute.
3. With the remaining batter, make seven more dosas in the same fashion, cooking each one on high for 1 minute on one side only. Add a little oil to the dish before cooking a fresh one. If necessary, brown the dosas under a conventional grill before serving.
4. If you are using a stuffing, place it in the middle of the uncooked side and fold the dosa up from both sides. Serve straight from the oven.

**Serves 4**

50 g/2 oz/½ cup black bean (urad) flour
100 g/4 oz/1 cup rice flour
½ teaspoon bicarbonate of soda
water, as required
½ teaspoon salt
oil, for greasing

**Prep 10 min**
**+ standing time 15 min**
**Cooking 10 min**

# Daalein

## LEGUMES OR PULSES

*Legumes or pulses are a great source of protein, fibre and vitamins. Cheap to buy and simple to cook, they are an integral part of a vegetarian main meal in India and the daal dishes are thus something of an institution in the Indian food firmament.*

*The pulses can be used whole or split, with their skin or hulled (skinless). There is a staggering range of legumes available in the market place.*

*Depending on your personal preference, the finished texture of the pulse preparations can be dry, thick as purée, thin as curry or thinner-still, like soups. When used in powder or ground-paste forms, together with other ingredients, legumes produce stunning delicacies.*

*The dry daal preparations can be served with salads or used for stuffing; the purées can be served alongside vegetables with dry meat dishes such as chops and cutlets; the thin variety is normally served with boiled rice or chapatty; and the further-thinned variety is used to make heartwarming soups.*

*Although legendary, pulse dishes are notorious for taking too long to cook. Generally speaking, peas take the longest; next come the beans and lastly, others like lentils take the least time to cook. Whole pulses take longer than the skinless and split varieties as the skin on whole pulses prevents the penetration of moisture.*

*Yet the microwave has changed traditional perceptions and practices. Daals take less time to cook, they cook flawlessly and taste great. All pulses benefit from a good soak prior to cooking, particularly the whole daals, as soaking loosens their skin, allowing them to expand more rapidly without falling apart.*

# Toor (Arhar Ki) Daal

PIGEON PEA PURÉE

**Serves 4**

225 g/8 oz/1 cup pigeon
  peas
600 ml/1 pint/2½ cups
  lukewarm water
1 teaspoon turmeric powder
salt, to taste
½ lemon
2-3 tablespoons caramelized
  onions (see p. 32),
  reheated

**Prep 5 min
+ soaking time
Cooking 20 min
+ standing time 10 min**

*Among the daals, this one is the most popular. It is rich in protein and simple to cook, although it is notorious for taking too long to cook. The easiest way round this problem is to pre-soak the peas, which almost halves the cooking time. In the microwave, toor daal cooks to perfection.*

1. Pick over and wash the pigeon peas then soak them for at least 4 hours in warm water (or overnight in normal tap water). Drain off the water and set aside.
2. In a microwave-safe casserole of 2.4 litre/4 pint/10 cup capacity, place the peas, measured water, turmeric and salt. Cook, uncovered, at full power for 20 minutes, or until the daal is tender and is blending with the water. Stir a couple of times during cooking, removing any scum forming at the top.
3. Remove from the oven, cover with a tight-fitting lid and leave to stand for 10 minutes to complete the cooking process. Uncover, squeeze the lemon over the dish and serve, garnished with the reheated onion mixture. Serve with a boiled rice or a chapatty.

# Khatti Masoor Daal

LENTILS IN LIME

*There is a Hindi saying: 'Yeh munh aur daal masoor ki?' Roughly translated, it means that you have to have a special type of mouth before you are entitled to savour this great dish. It is really good. Adjust the consistency by adding more water if desired, after the first stage.*

1. Pick over and wash the lentils in cold, running water. Drain and place in a microwave-compatible dish. Add the measured water and salt and cook, uncovered, at full power for 15
minutes, or until the lentils are soft, and the water has been absorbed. Stir a couple of times during cooking.
2. Remove the daal from the oven, stir in the lemon juice, cover and leave it to stand for 5 minutes. Stir before serving laced with the glazed mustard.

Serves 4

225 g/8 oz/1 cup lentils (masoor)
600 ml/1 pint/2½ cups warm water
salt, to taste
2-3 tablespoons lemon juice
glazed mustard (see p. 34)

Prep 5 min
Cooking 15 min
+ standing time 5 min

# Basanti Moong Daal

GREEN BEANS IN TURMERIC

Serves 4

225 g/8 oz/1 cup skinless,
   split mung beans
1 teaspoon turmeric powder
salt, to taste
600 ml/1 pint/2½ cups warm
   water
1 tablespoon lemon juice
2-3 tablespoons caramelized
   onions (see p.32),
   reheated

Prep 5 min
+ soaking time
Cooking 12 min
+ standing time 5 min

*Cooking this dish in a microwave is really great: no constant attendance, no stirring and the beans come out plump and juicy. The preparation is light on the stomach and the turmeric gives it a golden glow. Adjust the amount of liquid (and cooking time) to your liking.*

1. Pick over and wash the beans then soak them in warm water for 4 hours. Drain and set aside.

2. In a microwave-proof bowl of 1.8 litre/3 pint/7½ cup capacity, place the beans, turmeric, salt and water. Cook, half-covered, on high for 10 minutes, or until the beans are soft and most of the water has either been absorbed or evaporated.

3. Stir in the lemon juice and continue to cook, covered, at full power for another 2 minutes. Remove from the oven and leave, covered, to stand for 5 minutes. Stir in the reheated onion mixture and serve as required.

# Sookhi Urad Daal

DRY BLACK BEANS

*Some people prefer this dish to have a liquid consistency (in which case, adjust the water and cooking time accordingly). The beauty of this dish is that it remains thick and all the daal seeds separate. Serve as part of a main meal.*

1. Pick over the beans and soak them in warm water for 2 hours or so. Drain off the water and set aside.
2. Place the beans, asafoetida, turmeric, measured water and salt in a microwave-safe casserole of 1.8 litre/3 pint/7½ cup capacity. Half-cover with the lid and cook at full power for 16 minutes, or until the water has been absorbed and the beans are soft. Stir a couple of times during cooking. Remove from the oven and leave to stand, covered, for 5 minutes.
3. Meanwhile, place the ghee, onion, garlic, cumin and chillies in a skillet and microwave at full power for 3 minutes, stirring once halfway through cooking. Serve the daal in individual bowls and spoon a quarter of the onion mixture over each one.

Serves 4

225 g/8 oz/1 cup skinless split black beans (urad daal)
pinch of asafoetida powder
½ teaspoon turmeric powder
600 ml/1 pint/2½ cups warm water
salt, to taste
2 tablespoons ghee
2 tablespoons finely chopped onion
2 cloves garlic, crushed
1 teaspoon white cumin seeds
½ teaspoon crushed red chillies

Prep 10 min
+ soaking time
Cooking 19 min
+ standing time 5 min

# Khat-Mitthi Panchratni Daal

## SWEET AND SOUR MIXED PULSES

**Serves 4**

225 g/8 oz/1 cup
  mixed pulses,
  such as black and green
  beans, pigeon peas, grams
  and lentils
600 ml/1 pint/2½ cups warm
  water
1 teaspoon turmeric powder
salt, to taste
pinch of asafoetida powder
2 teaspoons brown sugar
green mango slices, fresh or
  dried, to taste, or
  1 tablespoon lemon juice
1 teaspoon red chilli powder
2 tablespoons sautéed cumin
  (see p.33), reheated

**Prep 5 min**
**+ soaking time**
**Cooking 16 min**
**+ standing time 5 min**

*People from the Maharashtra state are partial to this sweet-'n'sour daal, a tasty, multi-coloured concoction. Feel free to substitute pulses of your choice. This preparation can be dry (purée consistency), or thin like a curry. Adjust the liquid to your taste (not forgetting to adjust the cooking time, too). Serve as part of a main meal.*

1. Pick over and wash the pulses in several changes of water then leave to soak overnight. Next day, drain off the water.
2. Place the pulses, measured water, turmeric and salt in a microwave-proof casserole 1.8 litre/3 pint/7½ cup capacity. Cook, half-covered, at full power for 8 minutes. Stir a couple of times during cooking and skim as necessary.
3. Add the remaining ingredients, apart from the cumin mixture. Cook, half-covered, at full power for another 8 minutes, or until the pulses are tender and have absorbed the water (add further water at this stage, if the preparation is too dry for you).
4. Remove from the oven and leave, fully covered, to stand for 5 minutes. Uncover, spoon the hot cumin mixture over the daal and serve.

# Masaali Saabut Moong

SPICY WHOLE MUNG BEANS

*The microwave cooks these whole green beans flawlessly. As if by magic, the beans expand enormously into large, moist, plump and meaty nuggets. Despite repeated heating, the beans don't crack, burst or fall apart. Cooking times will vary, depending on the moisture content of the beans.*

1. Pick over and wash the mung beans and soak overnight, or for at least 4 hours, in warm water. Drain and set aside.
2. Place the beans and half of the measured water in a microwave-proof covered dish casserole of 1.8 litre/3 pint/7½ cup capacity. Cover and cook at full power for 8 minutes or until all or most of the water has been absorbed.
3. Take the casserole out of the oven and add the rest of the measured water together with the turmeric, garlic, ginger, mango powder (or lemon juice) and salt. Replace the lid, return the casserole to the microwave and continue to cook at full power for another 8 minutes, or until the beans are soft and plump. If necessary, cook longer and add a little more water.
4. Remove the beans from the oven and stir in the reheated onion mixture. Cover and leave to stand for 5 minutes. Stir before serving with rice or bread in the company of a salad, chutney or pickle of your choice.

Serves 4

225 g/8 oz/1 cup dried whole mung beans
600 ml/1 pint/2½ cups warm water
½ teaspoon turmeric powder
4 cloves garlic, crushed
1 teaspoon grated root ginger
2 teaspoons mango powder (amchoor), or 1 teaspoon lemon juice
salt, to taste
2 tablespoons caramelized onions (see p.32), reheated

Prep 5 min
+ soaking time
Cooking 16 min
+ standing time 5 min

# Lobhiya Kajraare Nayan

PLUMP BLACK-EYED PEAS

Serves 4

225 g/8 oz/1 cup dried
   black-eyed peas
600 ml/1 pint/2½ cups warm
   water
pinch of asafoetida powder
½ teaspoon turmeric powder
4 cloves garlic, crushed
1½ teaspoons salt, or to
   taste
1 tablespoon lemon juice
2 tablespoons caramelized
   onions (see p.32), reheated

Prep 10 min
+ soaking time
Cooking 23 min
+ standing time 10 min

*Black-eyed peas (lobhiya) – or beans – can be bought fresh or dried. Fresh ones require less cooking time; I find the dried variety are always available and more reliable. They are variously regarded as a pulse or vegetable. This dish should be overcooked rather than undercooked; the peas will still not become mushy. Cooking times may vary, depending on the peas.*

1. Pick over and thoroughly wash the peas then soak them in water overnight. Drain off the water in the morning and set the peas aside.
2. In a microwave-compatible casserole of 2.4 litre/4 pint/10 cup capacity, place the measured water and peas together with the asafoetida, turmeric, garlic and salt. Cook, half-covered, on high for 18 minutes, stirring a couple of times during cooking.
3. When most of the water has soaked into the peas, they should have become soft and plump but not mushy. Check their state, add more water if necessary (this will vary according to the moisture content of the peas) and cook, covered, at full power for another 5 minutes.
4. Remove the casserole from the oven, uncover, stir the mixture and sprinkle the lemon juice and reheated onion mixture over the top. Re-cover and leave to stand for 10 minutes. Serve hot, with rice, salad and other side dishes of your choice.

# Urad Daal Saag-Pahetaa

## SPINACH AND BLACK BEANS

*Spinach gives body and muscle to this daal and does the digestive system no harm. Adjust the quantity of ginger, chilli and garlic to your taste.*

1. Pick over the beans and soak them in warm water for at least 2 hours. Meanwhile, wash the spinach leaves, coarsely chop them and set aside.
2. In a microwave-friendly casserole of 2.4 litre/4 pint/10 cup capacity, place the measured water, black beans, turmeric, asafoetida and salt. Cook, uncovered, at full power for 8 minutes, stirring a couple of times during cooking and skimming as necessary.
3. Remove the casserole from the oven and stir in the spinach, ginger and chillies. Continue cooking, half-covered, at full power for another 8 minutes. Remove the casserole from the oven, stir once or twice and leave to stand, fully covered, for 5 minutes.
4. Meanwhile, in a suitable skillet or bowl, place the ghee, onion, garlic and cumin. Cook, covered, at full power for 3 minutes. Add the onion mixture to the beans and serve hot with a little melted butter on each individual serving.

Serves 4

225 g/8 oz/1 cup split black beans (urad daal)
225 g/8 oz spinach
600 ml/1 pint/2½ cups warm water
½ teaspoon turmeric powder
pinch of asafoetida powder
salt, to taste
1 tablespoon grated root ginger
2 large dried red chillies, crushed
2 tablespoons ghee
2 tablespoons chopped onion
8 cloves garlic, crushed
1 teaspoon white cumin seeds
50 g/2 oz/¼ cup butter, melted

Prep 10 min
+ soaking and melting times
Cooking 19 min
+ standing time 5 min

# Daalein aur Lauki

## PULSES WITH MARROW

Serves 4

100 g/4 oz/ ½ cup hulled and split black beans (urad daal)
100 g/4 oz/½ cup hulled and split grams (chanaa daal)
1 small marrow (lauki), about 450 g/1 lb
900 ml/1½ pints/3¾ cups warm water
1½ teaspoons salt, or to taste
1 teaspoon turmeric powder
4 cloves garlic, chopped
1 tablespoon cooking oil
1 tablespoon chopped onion
pinch of asafoetida powder
1 teaspoon white cumin seeds
8 small dried red chillies, or 4 green chillies, chopped
½ lemon
2 tablespoons chopped coriander leaves

Prep 10 min
+ soaking time
Cooking 26 min
+ standing time 5 min

*This is a potent and delightful dish. If you prefer, the main ingredients can be replaced by, say, split peas and cucumber. Serve with rice or bread.*

1. Pick over then wash and soak both pulses in warm water for at least 2 hours. Drain off the water and set the pulses aside. Peel and chop the marrow into 1.25cm/½ inch round slices. Set aside.

2. In a microwave-proof casserole of 2.4 litre/4 pint/10 cup capacity, place the pulses, measured water, salt, turmeric and garlic. Cook, uncovered, at full power for 15 minutes, or until the pulses are soft. Stir from time to time, skimming as necessary.

3. Drop the marrow slices into the cooking pulses, half-cover and cook at medium power for another 8 minutes, or until the marrow is tender. Add some more water if the mixture becomes too dry for you.

4. Once the pulses and the marrow have blended (the marrow should not completely disappear into the pulses), remove the casserole from the oven and let it stand, fully covered, for 5 minutes.

5. Meanwhile, put the oil, onion, asafoetida and cumin in a microwavable skillet or bowl, and cook, uncovered, at full power for 3 minutes. Uncover the casserole and stir in the onion mixture. Squeeze the lemon over the top, scatter with coriander and serve.

# Dhansak

## PULSES WITH VEGETABLES

*Dhansak is a Parsee speciality. Parsees are people of Persian extraction living in India. The word dhansak means of high pedigree or quality. The dish can be non-vegetarian (with meat or chicken), or vegetarian, like this one. Among the vegetables, you may wish to include those of the leafy variety. Feel free to select your own garnish, such as caramelized onions or garam masala.*

1. Pick over and rinse the pulses in several changes of water then soak in some warm water for at least 2 hours. Drain and set aside.
2. Place the water and pulses in a microwave-proof casserole. Cook, uncovered, at full power for 8 minutes.
3. Stir in the vegetables, turmeric and salt and microwave, half-covered, at full power for another 7 minutes.
4. Add the ghee, cover fully, and continue cooking on high for another 5 minutes, or until the pulses are soft.
5. Remove the pulses from the oven, sprinkle them with the lemon juice and scatter the coriander leaves over the top. Cover and leave to stand for 5 minutes. Stir before serving with the garnish of your choice and accompanied by boiled rice or bread.

Serves 4

225 g/8 oz/1 cup mixed pulses
600 ml/1 pint/2½ cups warm water
225 g/8 oz/½ cup diced mixed vegetables
½ teaspoon turmeric powder
salt, to taste
4 tablespoons/⅓ cup ghee
1 tablespoon lemon juice
2 tablespoons chopped coriander leaves

Prep 15 min
+ soaking time
Cooking 24 min
+ standing time 5 min

# Toor Daal Ka Pharaa

BREAD IN PIGEON PEAS

**Serves 4**

225 g/8 oz/1 cup pigeon peas
  (toor daal)
1.2 litres/2 pints/5 cups
  lukewarm water
100 g/4 oz/1 cup chapatty
  flour
1 teaspoon turmeric powder
1 tablespoon mango powder
  (aamchoor), or 2 teaspoons
  lemon juice
salt, to taste
50 g/2 oz/¼ cup ghee
1 tablespoon white cumin
  seeds
large pinch of red chilli
  powder
2 tablespoons chopped
  coriander leaves

**Prep 10 min**
**+ soaking time**
**Cooking 22 min**
**+ standing time 5 min**

*This particular combination is a complete two-in-one meal – very tasty and flavoursome too. You may substitute the toor daal with another one of your choice. Serve by itself, with a dry vegetable dish and salad, chutney or pickle.*

1. Wash the pigeon peas under running water then soak them in warm water for 4 hours.
2. Drain the pigeon peas and place them in a microwave-safe casserole with the measured water. Cook, uncovered, at full power for 10 minutes. Stir two or three times during the cooking period, skimming as necessary.
3. Meanwhile, sift the flour into a bowl and add just enough water to make a soft dough. Knead lightly and divide the mixture into eight portions. Roll out each one into a thin, round disc.
4. Add the turmeric, mango powder (or lemon juice) and salt to the cooking pigeon peas. Half-cover the casserole and continue cooking at full power for another 2 minutes.
5. Slide the raw flour discs into the cooking daal one at a time. Cover the casserole and cook on high for another 8 minutes, or until the bread and daal are cooked through.
6. Remove the casserole from the oven and stir with care. Cover and leave to stand for 5 minutes.
7. Meanwhile, place the ghee, cumin and chilli powder and microwave in a separate microwavable bowl, uncovered, at full power for 2 minutes, stirring once halfway through.
8. Remove the casserole's lid and spoon the ghee-mixture over the contents. Stir and serve hot, sprinkled with the chopped coriander.

# Shaakahaari Bhojan

VEGETARIAN DISHES

*The popularity of vegetarian diets has been on the ascendant for a long while now, and not just because of the health-foodies or weight-watchers. To be vegetarian is fast becoming the done thing. India has long been an international centre of vegetarianism. Over the centuries, Indian chefs have devised unusual and ingenious ways of cooking everyday vegetables like potatoes, peas or cauliflower. Indian vegetarian dishes are rich in fibre, proteins, iron and vitamins and are wholesome and sophisticated. These preparations combine vegetables, herbs, spices, legumes, fruits and milk products such as yoghurt and cream cheese to produce exotic and fragrant flavours.*

*Vegetables cooked in the microwave retain their shape (even aubergines), colour (carrots and peas become brighter), flavour (cauliflower's taste becomes more pronounced) and become pleasantly tender. These exotic, brightly coloured, vitamin-packed and flavoursome vegetables have an edge over their conventionally cooked kin in terms of time, but remember, a little standing time at the end of cooking leads to perfect results.*

*The Indian technique for cooking vegetables is two-fold: stir-cooking and steaming. The microwave handles this technique efficiently: stir-cooking requires less oil and reduces the need for stirring, while the steaming is done in a minimum of water. The finished dishes look and taste lighter and become perfectly tender in just a few minutes.*

*Aided by herbs, spices and a little imagination, you can create fantastic dishes with leftover cooked vegetables. These include foogaths (dry dishes made from curries and vice versa), salads and rice-mixed meals.*

# Paalak aur Paneer

## Spinach and Cream Cheese

Serves 4

225 g/8 oz/2 cups fresh
  spinach
225 g/8 oz/2 cups red and
  yellow peppers
2 tablespoons cooking oil
1 medium onion, finely
  chopped
4 medium tomatoes, finely
  chopped
pinch of asafoetida powder
2 teaspoons salt, or to taste
2 green chillies, finely
  chopped
225 g/8 oz/1 cup cream
cheese (see p.38)

Prep 10 min
Cooking 12 min
+ standing time 5 min

*The riot of colour in this dish is sheer magic to the eyes, and the taste is wondrous to the palate. Spinach and cream cheese are light on the stomach but the microwave somehow makes them taste lighter still! The green of spinach, when cooked in a microwave, manages to become even greener. In this dish, the spinach can be replaced by another green of your choice.*

1. Trim, rinse and chop the spinach and put it on a plate. Then take the peppers, core them (optional) and shred the flesh into long strips. Keep on a plate.
2. Place the oil and onion in a microwavable dish of 1.8 litre/3 pint/7½ cup capacity. Cover and cook at full power for 3 minutes, stirring once halfway through. Toss in the peppers, tomatoes, asafoetida and cook, covered, at full power for 2 minutes.
3. Remove the dish from the oven, uncover and add the spinach, stirring once or twice. Replace the lid and cook on high for 3 minutes, or until the spinach wilts.
4. Stir in the salt and green chillies and blend well then carefully fold in the cream cheese and cover with the lid. Cook on high for 4 minutes.
5. Remove the dish from the oven and leave to stand, covered, for 5 minutes. Stir with care before serving.

# Bhindi Bhaaji

FRIED OKRA

*Bhindi in English is okra or lady's fingers. This delicious dry vegetable preparation can be served as a side dish with a main meal or on its own with one of the bread dishes.*

1. Wash the okra and cut it into rounds, discarding the tops.
2. Place the oil in a microwave-safe dish and cook, covered, on high for 1 minute. Add the garlic and turmeric and blend well. Continue cooking, uncovered, for another 2 minutes.
3. Stir in the okra, onion and chillies, mixing thoroughly. Cook, uncovered, at full power for 6 minutes, stirring a couple of times during cooking.
4. Add the salt and mango powder or lemon juice and continue cooking, uncovered, at full power for another 5 minutes, stirring occasionally, until the okra is glazed.
5. Remove the okra from the oven and leave it to stand, covered, for 2 minutes. Serve hot, sprinkled with chopped coriander.

Serves 4

450 g/1 lb tender okra
2 tablespoons cooking oil
2 cloves garlic, chopped
½ teaspoon turmeric powder
1 medium onion, finely sliced
2 green chillies, chopped
salt, to taste
2 teaspoons mango powder
   (aamchoor), or 2 teaspoons
   lemon juice
2 tablespoons chopped
   coriander leaves

Prep 10 min
Cooking time 14 min
+ standing time 2 min

# Methi Ka Lahsuni Saag

## GREEN FENUGREEK BRAISED IN GARLIC

**Serves 4**

2 tablespoons mustard oil
6 cloves garlic, chopped
4 dried red chillies, crushed
225 g/8 oz/2 cups new
  potatoes, sliced
225 g/8 oz/2 cups fenugreek
  leaves
100 g/4 oz/1 cup green soya
  spears, chopped
salt, to taste

**Prep 10 min**
**Cooking 12 min**
**+ standing time 5 min**

*This must be one of the simplest dishes to cook in a microwave and it tastes super. Normally served as a side dish, with a main meal, it can also be served on its own with your choice of bread. Feel free to adjust the quantity of garlic and red chillies to suit your palate.*

1. Place the oil and garlic in a microwave-proof lidded casserole and cook, covered, at full power for 2 minutes. Add the chillies and cook for another 2 minutes, stirring once halfway through.
2. Remove the casserole from the oven and add the potatoes, stirring to coat them in the oil. Then add the fenugreek and soya, cover and cook on high for 5 minutes.
3. Take the casserole out, remove the lid and stir several times. The volume of the greens will be considerably reduced by now. Stir in the salt, return to the oven and cook, covered, at full power for another 3 minutes, or until the potatoes are soft.
4. Leave to stand, covered, for 5 minutes before serving.

# Boondi Kadhi

BATTER-DROP CURRY

Kadhi is the original Indian curry. The word kadhi
was corrupted during the British Raj and came to
be pronounced 'curry'. Inspired by that, all Indian
dishes with gravy or liquid came to be christened
'curry'. This particular version is best if the yoghurt
is on the sour side; you can use soured cream, or
add a teaspoon of lemon juice. Traditionally, kadhi
is made slightly differently to this: instead of boondi (batter drops), it is made with phuloris or plain
pakodas which are deep-fried (not possible in a
microwave oven) and takes longer to cook. Ready
boondi packets are easily available from most
Asian grocery outlets, so making kadhi in a
microwave becomes possible, easy and speedy.

1. In a deep bowl, whisk the yoghurt, gram flour and water
into a smooth batter.
2. Place the oil in a microwave-proof casserole of around 2.4
litre/4 pint/10 cup capacity. Heat, covered, at full power for 2
minutes, then stir in the mustard, asafoetida, turmeric and
half the chilli powder. Pour in the yoghurt mixture and salt
and cook, covered, for 8 minutes, or until the mixture comes
to a rolling boil. Stir a couple of times during cooking.
3. Add the batter drops to the yoghurt mixture and cook,
half-covered, at full power for 5 minutes, or until the mixture
is well blended. Stir once or twice during cooking.
4. Remove the mixture from the oven, sprinkle the
caramelized onion and the remaining chilli powder over the
top, cover and leave to stand for 5 minutes. Serve with boiled
rice or the bread of your choice.

Serves 4

300 ml/½ pint/1¼ cups plain
  yoghurt
2 tablespoons gram flour
  (besan)
600 ml/1 pint/2½ cups water
2 tablespoons cooking oil
1 tablespoon mustard seeds
pinch of asafoetida powder
large pinch of turmeric
  powder
1 teaspoon chilli powder
salt, to taste
100 g/4 oz/1 cup batter drops
  (boondi)
2-3 tablespoons caramelized
  onions (see p.32)

Prep 10 min
Cooking 15 min
+ standing time 5 min

# Shaahi Sabzi Quorma

ROYAL INDIAN KORMA

**Serves 4**

450 g/1 lb mixed vegetables
  such as aubergine, carrots,
  cauliflower, courgettes and
  peppers, cut into small
  pieces
salt, as required
3 tablespoons/¼ cup ghee
2 tablespoons chopped onion
2 cloves garlic, sliced
½ teaspoon grated root
  ginger
seeds of 4 green cardamoms
8 black peppercorns, crushed
2 tomatoes, sliced
2 green chillies, chopped
6 tablespoons/½ cup plain
  yoghurt
2 tablespoons double cream
2 teaspoons garam masala
2 tablespoons chopped
  coriander leaves

Prep 10 min
Cooking 18 min
+ standing time 5 min

*Quorma is the name for a mild genre of moist curries developed during the Mughal regime in India. Despite the Mughal penchant for meats, though, this particular dish is made from vegetables and in creating it I have endeavoured to bring about a happy amalgam of the southern dish avial with the northern quorma. Cooked in the microwave, the vegetables remain whole and retain their flavour and texture. Remember, the dish must be mild to your taste, so feel free to adjust the amount of chillies, spices and root ginger.*

1. Place the ghee, onion, garlic and ginger in a microwave-safe casserole and cook, covered, on high for 4 minutes, stirring halfway through.
2. Add the cardamom seeds and peppercorns and mix well. Then add the tomatoes, green chillies and yoghurt and blend thoroughly. Cook, covered, at full power for another 4 minutes.
3. Stir in the vegetables, cream and salt to taste and mix well. Cook, covered, at full power for another 10 minutes, or until the vegetables are tender. Stir once or twice during cooking.
4. Sprinkle the mixture with the garam masala and coriander. Cover and leave to stand for 5 minutes before serving.

# Matar Paneer

## CREAM CHEESE AND GREEN PEAS

*This dainty curry embellishes a meatless meal without hassle but also goes well on its own with a bread or rice preparation. Although an offering from the Punjab region, matar paneer has gained universal popularity.*

1. Grind the coriander seeds, garlic and half the onion into a paste.

2. Place the ghee and cream cheese in a microwavable casserole, cover and cook on high for 2 minutes. Carefully turn over the cheese halfway through cooking. Remove and drain the cheese on a plate.

3. Add the remaining onion, plus the ginger and bay leaves to the ghee still in the casserole. Stir and microwave, uncovered, at full power for 3 minutes, or until the onion is opaque. Stir halfway through cooking. Add the turmeric and herb paste, cover and microwave at full power for 5 minutes, stirring once.

4. Add the peas, cheese, yoghurt, chillies, tomatoes and salt and stir thoroughly. Cover and cook at full power for 3 minutes.

5. Pour in the water and continue microwaving at full power for another 5 minutes, or until the water begins to boil. Remove the casserole from the oven and leave to stand, covered, for 5 minutes.

6. Stir in the garam masala and serve sprinkled with coriander.

Serves 4

1 tablespoon coriander seeds
6 cloves garlic, crushed
2 medium onions, chopped
100 g/4 oz/½ cup ghee
225 g/8 oz/1 cup cream
  cheese (see p.38), diced
1 tablespoon grated root
  ginger
1 teaspoon turmeric powder
450 g/1lb green peas
150 ml/¼ pint/⅔ cup plain
  yoghurt
2 green chillies, chopped
225 g/8 oz/2 cups tomatoes,
  sliced
salt, to taste
450 ml/¾ pint water
2 teaspoons garam masala
2 tablespoons chopped
  coriander leaves

Prep 15 min
Cooking 18 min
+ standing time 5 min

# Matar Keema

MINCED PEAS

**Serves 4**

275 g/10 oz/1¾ cups green
  peas
4 tablespoons cooking oil
1 teaspoon grated fresh root
  ginger
2 medium potatoes, finely
  chopped
2 bay leaves
2 medium onions, chopped
2 medium tomatoes, chopped
2 teaspoons salt, or to taste
300 ml/½ pint/1¼ cups
  water
2 teaspoons garam masala,
  to garnish
2 tablespoons chopped
  coriander leaves, to garnish

**For the spice paste:**
4 cloves garlic, crushed
1 teaspoon grated root ginger
1 teaspoon turmeric powder
1 teaspoon red chilli powder
2 tablespoons coriander
  seeds

Prep 20 min
Cooking 26 min
+ standing time 5 min

*Undoubtedly, this rather unusual vegetarian dish
will also find favour with meat eaters. It is moist
and exquisite – a particular favourite of mine. Serve
it with a rice pullao or the bread of your choice.*

1. Make the spice paste by grinding together the garlic,
ginger, turmeric, chilli powder and coriander seeds until
smooth. Set aside. Coarsely grind the peas and set them
aside separately.
2. Place 1 tablespoon of the oil in a microwavable dish and
heat, covered, at full power for 2 minutes. Add the ginger and
peas, stir then replace the lid and cook at full power for 3
minutes, or until the pea-grains begin to separate. Stir once
or twice during cooking. Remove from the oven and set
aside, still covered.
3. In another microwave-safe dish, place 1 tablespoon of the
oil and the chopped potatoes and cook, covered, at full
power for 3 minutes, stirring once. Remove from the oven
and mix with the peas.
4. Place the remaining oil in one of the cooking dishes and
heat, covered, on high for 2 minutes. Add the bay leaves and
onion and cook, covered, at full power for another 3 minutes,
or until the onion becomes opaque. Stir in the tomatoes and
the spice paste, and continue cooking, covered, on high for 5
minutes, stirring a couple of times.
5. Remove the dish from the oven, stir in the pea-and-potato
mixture, salt and measured water. Return to the microwave
and cook, uncovered, at full power for another 8 minutes,
stirring occasionally.
6. Sprinkle the garam masala over the dish then scatter with
the coriander leaves. Cover and leave to stand for 5 minutes.
Stir before serving.

# Malaai Chanaa aur Khumbi

## CREAMED GRAMS AND MUSHROOMS

*Making a curry out of chick peas (garbanzos) is a little unusual, to say the least, but when cooked with mushrooms, this dish becomes celestial! The juices released by the mushrooms join the onion, garlic and cream to produce a creamy gravy which tastes out of this world. The mushrooms themselves absorb some of the gravy and become plump and scrumptious. All in all, this curry has excellent credentials.*

1. Soak the pulses in cold water overnight. Next day, rinse them under a tap then drain thoroughly and discard any hard ones. Crush half of the remaining ones, leaving the rest whole.
2. Heat the oil in a microwave-compatible dish, uncovered, at full power for 2 minutes. Stir in the onion, turmeric, garam masala, garlic, ginger and chillies. Continue cooking, uncovered, on high for another 3 minutes, stirring once.
3. Add the ground and whole pulses and stir well. Cover and cook on high for 3 minutes, then stir in the mushrooms and cook, covered, for another 2 minutes.
4. Stir in the yoghurt, soured cream, measured water and salt. Half-cover the dish and cook at full power for 10 minutes, or until the chick peas (garbanzos) are soft.
5. Remove the curry from the oven, sprinkle with the coconut and black pepper and leave, fully covered, to stand for 5 minutes. Serve with a bread or rice dish.

Serves 4

225 g/8 oz/1 cup dried chick peas (garbanzo beans)
2 tablespoons cooking oil
2 medium onions, finely chopped
1 teaspoon turmeric powder
2 teaspoons garam masala
4 cloves garlic, crushed
1 teaspoon grated root ginger
2 green chillies, chopped
225 g/8 oz/2 cups button mushrooms, halved
300 ml/½ pint/1¼ cups plain yoghurt
2 tablespoons soured cream
300 ml/½ pint/1¼ cups water
salt, to taste
2 tablespoons desiccated coconut
pinch of freshly ground black pepper

Prep 10 min
+ soaking time
Cooking 20 min
+ standing time 5 min

# Makhaane Rasedaar

LOTUS PUFFS IN PEA SAUCE

Serves 4

2 tablespoons cooking oil
50 g/2 oz lotus puffs, halved
1 small onion, finely chopped
1 clove garlic, sliced
350 g/12 oz green peas,
   ground
1 green chilli, chopped
1 teaspoon grated root ginger
300 ml/½ pint/1¼ cups
   water
2 teaspoons salt, or to taste
pinch of green cardamom
   powder
2 teaspoons mango
   powder (aamchoor), or
   1 teaspoon lemon juice
1 teaspoon garam masala

Prep 10 min
Cooking 16 min
+ standing time 5 min

*The exquisite taste of this curry will find favour with diners of all persuasions. It should be moist when ready, but do feel free to adjust the quantitiy of liquid – there is much scope for experimentation in this recipe.*

1. Place 2 teaspoons of the oil in a microwave-safe dish of 1.8 litre/3 pint/7½ cup capacity and heat at full power for 2 minutes. Add the halved lotus puffs and cook, uncovered, for 1 minute, stirring halfway through. Transfer the lotus puffs to a plate and set aside.

2. Pour the remaining oil into the cooking dish, add the onion and garlic and cook, uncovered, at full power for 3 minutes, or until the onion is opaque.

3. Stir in the ground peas, chilli and ginger, cover and cook on high for 3 minutes, stirring once or twice. Add the lotus puffs, measured water and salt and cook, half-covered, at full power for 5 minutes.

4. Stir the cardamom and mango powders (or lemon juice) into the mixture and cook for another 2 minutes. Stir in the garam masala, replace the lid and leave to stand for 5 minutes before serving.

# Kele Ke Chatpatay Kofte

SPICY PLANTAIN KOFTAS

*This delicious offering comes to you from the Indian kofta artistes. It will surely be a valuable addition to your culinary repertoire. Serve with a rice or bread dish. For variety, you may replace the plantain with snakegourd (lauki).*

1. In a deep, microwavable bowl, place the plantains and add sufficient water to submerge them. Cook, uncovered, on high for 4 minutes then leave to cool.

2. Peel and mash the plantains and place the flesh in a large bowl. Add the flour, salt, chilli, onion and garlic and knead into a smooth mixture. Greasing the palms of your hands with ghee, shape the mixture into small balls.

3. Spread the breadcrumbs on a platter and roll each ball (kofta) over the breadcrumbs until evenly coated. Place the koftas on a greased microwave-safe flat dish and cook, uncovered, at full power for 4 minutes, turning over once in between. Remove the dish from the oven and set aside.

4. Take a microwave-friendly casserole of 1.2 litre/2 pint/5 cup capacity. Pour in the ready gravy and cook, uncovered, at full power for 4 minutes, or until the gravy comes to a boil. Carefully drop the koftas into the gravy, cover and continue cooking on high for 3 minutes.

5. Remove the casserole from the oven, uncover and sprinkle with the garam masala. Replace the lid and let the dish stand for 5 minutes. Give it a careful stir then serve.

Serves 4

4 plantains
50 g/2 oz/½ cup wholemeal flour
2 green chillies, chopped
1 small onion, finely chopped
1 clove garlic, chopped
ghee, as necessary
breadcrumbs, for coating
300 ml/½ pint/1¼ cups vegetarian ready gravy (see p.35)
1 teaspoon garam masala
salt

Prep 10 min
Cooking 15 min
+ standing time 5 min

# Shaljum Bhurta

MASHED TURNIP

Serves 4

450 g/1 lb turnips
2 tablespoons oil
1 teaspoon grated root
  ginger
1 medium onion, finely
  chopped
2 medium tomatoes,
  quartered
2 green chillies, chopped
½ teaspoon cumin powder
1 teaspoon garam masala
salt, to taste
1 tablespoon chopped
  coriander leaves

Prep 10 min
Cooking 14 min
+ standing time 2 min

*Bhurtas are mashed vegetables. They are made quickly, have a pungent taste and look appetizing. Acquire a taste for these dishes and you are hooked for ever! You can make a similar bhurta with aubergines.*

1. Place the turnips in a microwave-safe casserole, cover and cook at full power for 5 minutes, or until the turnips are tender. Leave covered until cool, then peel and mash the turnips.
2. Place the oil in a suitable flat dish, together with the ginger and onion. Cook, covered, at full power for 4 minutes, stirring once halfway through.
3. Add the tomatoes, chillies, cumin and garam masala. Then stir in the mashed turnip, add salt and blend thoroughly. Microwave, uncovered, on high for 5 minutes, stirring a couple of times during cooking.
4. Remove the dish from the oven and leave to stand for 2 minutes to complete the cooking process. Top with the coriander leaves and serve.

# Aalu Bhurta

MASHED POTATO

*Nothing like its Western namesake, this quickly prepared, multicoloured dish is not just a pretty face, it tastes pretty wonderful too!*

1. Having first pricked the potatoes all over, place them in a microwave-safe casserole, with enough water to submerge them. Cover and cook at full power for 5 minutes or until the potatoes are soft. Remove from the oven and leave covered until cool. Then peel and mash the potatoes.
2. Place half the ghee in a flat dish, together with the onion and garlic and microwave, covered, on high for 4 minutes, stirring halfway through.
3. Add the potatoes, tomatoes, garam masala, chilli powder, ginger and salt and blend together. Cook, uncovered, at full power for 5 minutes, stirring occasionally.
4. Remove from the oven, sprinkle with the remaining ghee and stir. Garnish with the coriander leaves, cover and leave to stand for 2 minutes. Stir before serving.

Serves 4

450 g/1 lb potatoes
4 tablespoons/⅓ cup ghee
4 spring onions, chopped
2 cloves garlic, sliced
4 tomatoes, chopped
1 teaspoon garam masala
1 teaspoon red chilli powder
1 teaspoon grated root ginger
salt, to taste
2 tablespoons chopped
    coriander leaves

Prep 10 min
Cooking 14 min
+ standing time 2 min

# Bharwaan Baigan

STUFFED AUBERGINES

Serves 4

4 long aubergines/eggplants
    about 450 g/1 lb in total
1 tablespoon fenugreek
    seeds
1 tablespoon fennel seeds
1 tablespoon cumin seeds
1 tablespoon coriander seeds
1 teaspoon turmeric powder
1 tablespoon mango
    powder (aamchoor), or
    1 tablespoon lemon juice
1 teaspoon red chilli powder
2 teaspoons salt, or to taste
150 ml/¼ pint/⅔ cup
    cooking oil
2 tablespoons thinly sliced
    onion

Prep 10 min
Cooking 14 min
+ standing time 2 min

*The Indian cookery repertoire has a long list of stuffed dishes and offers wide scope for experimentation. The vegetarian fillings are similar for most dishes of this ilk. The elongated variety of aubergine is preferable for this particular preparation. With some adjustments, you can make a similar dish with okra (lady's fingers) or green chillies.*

1. Keeping intact the leafy sepals at the top of the aubergines, slit them lengthways without fully halving them.
2. Spread the fenugreek, fennel, cumin and coriander seeds on a microwavable plate and roast, uncovered, at full power for 3 minutes, or until the spices become several shades darker and exude an aromatic smell. Cool, then grind them into a fine powder.
3. To the ground spices, add the turmeric, mango powder (or lemon juice), chilli and salt and mix well. Pour in a little oil to make the mixture binding (there is no need for oil if you are using lemon juice instead of mango powder). Stuff the mixture into the aubergines, reserving the leftover mixture for later use.
4. Place the remaining oil and onion in a microwave-safe skillet and cook, covered, on high for 3 minutes, or until the onions look glazed.
5. Arrange the aubergines on the bed of onion, scatter the leftover spice mixture around the aubergines and cook, covered, at full power for 8 minutes, or until the aubergines are tender. Turn the aubergines over twice during this cooking period.
6. Remove the dish from the oven and leave to stand, covered, for 2 minutes. Uncover and serve hot or cold, with a main meal or with bread.

# Bharwaan Tamaatar

## CAPPED TOMATOES

*A very colourful and popular dish. The filling can be varied to suit your personal taste. You can similarly make stuffed peppers.*

1. Slice the tops from the tomatoes and scoop out the pulp. Reserve the tops and pulp for later.
2. In a microwave-safe bowl, place the diced vegetables and sufficient water to submerge them. Cook, half-covered, at full power for 2 minutes. Remove from the oven and set aside, fully covered.
3. Meanwhile, on a large plate, mix half of the coriander leaves with the chillies, onion, ginger, garam masala and salt, and mix well. Stir in the tomato-pulp and diced vegetables then use this mixture to stuff the tomato shells. Cover with the tomato tops and secure with cocktail sticks.
4. Place 2 tablespoons cooking oil on a flat dish and add the cumin. Cover and cook at full power for 2 minutes. Remove the cover, arrange the tomatoes over the cumin and sprinkle the leftover filling mixture around the tomatoes. Re-cover and cook on high for 8 minutes, or until the tomatoes lose their raw look and seem glazed. Turn the tomatoes over, ever so carefully, halfway through the cooking period.
5. Remove the dish from the oven and sprinkle the remaining chopped coriander leaves over the top. Replace the lid and leave to stand for 5 minutes. Remove the cocktail sticks before serving.

Serves 4

4 firm, ripe tomatoes
4 tablespoons diced mixed
  vegetables
2 tablespoons chopped
  coriander leaves
2 green chillies, chopped
1 small onion, finely chopped
pinch of grated root ginger
1 teaspoon garam masala
salt, to taste
cooking oil, as necessary
1 teaspoon white cumin
  seeds

Prep 10 min
Cooking 12 min
+ standing time 5 mins

# Dum Aalu

## WHOLE POTATOES

**Serves 4**

16 small potatoes, about
225 g/8 oz/2 cups in total
1 small onion, grated
1.5 cm/½ inch piece root
ginger, crushed
2 green chillies, chopped
2 cloves garlic, halved
3 tablespoons/¼ cup oil
pinch of turmeric powder
2 bay leaves
150 ml/¼ pint/⅔ cup plain
yoghurt
salt, to taste
1 teaspoon garam masala
2 tablespoons chopped
coriander leaves

Prep 10 min
+ soaking time
Cooking 14 min
+ standing time 5 min

*This scrumptious side-dish is a hot favourite of the Pandya family. Serve on its own with a bread, or with rice in the main meal.*

1. Scrape the potatoes, prick them all over with a fork and soak in salted water for 30 minutes. Remove and wash thoroughly under a tap, then pat dry.
2. Meanwhile, make a paste by grinding together the onion, ginger, chillies and garlic, and set aside.
3. Place half the oil in a microwave-safe casserole. Add the potatoes, cover and microwave on high for 4 minutes, stirring once halfway through. Drain and set aside.
4. Add the remaining oil to the casserole, together with the turmeric, bay leaves and spice paste. Stir thoroughly and cook, covered, at full power for 2 minutes. Stir in the yoghurt and salt and continue to cook, covered, on high for another 2 minutes.
5. Stir the potatoes into the casserole, cover and cook at full power for 6 minutes, or until the potatoes are soft. Halfway through the cooking period, stir carefully, add a splash of water if the mixture looks too dry and sprinkle with the garam masala.
6. Remove the casserole from the oven, stir and leave to stand, covered, for 5 minutes. Scatter the coriander over the potatoes and serve hot or cold.

# Shobhi Gobhi

## GLORIOUS WHOLE CAULIFLOWER

*The whole or musallam dishes are a Mughal bequest to Indian cuisine. They are usually served with the main meal, in the company of several other dishes. Take the time to enjoy the visual appeal of this stunning concoction before the eating starts!*

1.Trim the hard outer leaves from the cauliflower and remove the stem. Add a pinch of salt to the lemon juice and rub this mixture all over the cauliflower.

2. Place the cauliflower, face down, in a suitable microwave-safe casserole and cook, covered, at full power for 10 minutes, or until the cauliflower is tender, but still shipshape (cooking times will vary considerably according to the moisture content and size of the cauliflower). Remove from the oven and transfer the cauliflower on to a plate.

3. In the same casserole, place the oil and tomato and cook at full power for 2 minutes. Add the ready gravy, chilli powder and green chillies, if using. Cover and cook on high for 4 minutes, or until the gravy comes to a boil.

4. In a separate lidded casserole, sit the cauliflower face up. Carefully pour the boiling gravy all over the cauliflower, sprinkle with garam masala and cover. Microwave at full power for another 2 minutes.

5. Remove from the oven and leave the casserole to stand, covered, for 5 minutes. Transfer the contents to a serving dish, arrange the lemon slices around the cauliflower, scatter with coriander and serve.

**Serves 4**

1 medium cauliflower, about 675 g/1½ lb
salt, as required
2 tablespoons lemon juice
2 tablespoons cooking oil
2 tomatoes, chopped
600 ml/1 pint/2½ cups vegetarian ready gravy (see p.35)
½ teaspoon red chilli powder
2 fresh green chillies, chopped (optional)
2 teaspoons garam masala
lemon slices, to garnish
coriander leaves, to garnish

**Prep 10 min**
**Cooking 18 min**
**+ standing time 5 min**

# Gosht, Murghi, Machhli

MEAT, POULTRY, FISH

*The population of India is divided roughly half-and-half between vegetarians and non-vegetarians. The non-vegetarian sector of Indian cuisine consists of a variety of juicy and tender delicacies made with meat, poultry and fish. The red meats commonly used in India are goat or lamb. Because of religious taboos, beef and pork dishes tend to be highly regionalized.*

*The microwave provides an ideal environment for cooking Indian meat dishes. Its moist and trapped heat tenderizes and cooks meat speedily and takes less than half of the conventional cooking times. Meat absorbs the flavour of herbs and spices and comes out fragrant and succulent, with a velvety texture.*

*The microwaves penetrate no more than 3.75 cm / 1½ inch from the surface of the food, so pieces of meat should be small and uniform for best results. When the fat is trimmed off (fat absorbs microwaves and delays cooking) and no more than a little fat is added to cooking, the dish is lower in calories and cholesterol.*

*As for poultry, the meat is usually skinned and marinated before cooking, which enables the spices to permeate the flesh and to tenderize and flavour the meat. Chicken is rich in protein and very popular all over India. It is highly suited to cooking in the moist heat of the microwave; considerable cooking time is saved and it is difficult to overcook the chicken, particularly if it is cooking in gravy. The same goes for duck.*

*Chicken also absorbs well the flavour of herbs and spices, and marinating it does wonders. The result is delicious and succulent. Given that virtually no oil is required for tandoori preparations or* braising, microwave cooking leads to a low-calorie, low-fat poultry dishes.

Besides meat and poultry, Indians have access to some 2,000 varieties of fish. India is surrounded by water on three sides and boasts large lakes and enormous rivers. The coastal regions are particularly noted for their wonderful fish and other seafood preparations.

The microwave oven is handy to braise and other-wise cook fish dishes quickly – many are ready within 15 minutes and the fish retain their shape and flavour. Most fish dishes can be reheated with-out becoming hard or dry however, given the small amount of time required to cook fish, it is advisable to cook them fresh each time.

# Chhappar Kabaab

THATCHER KEBABS

*The thatcher provides happiness to his family by thatching the roof of their house. Similarly, these kebabs delight the hungry diners of his household, hence the soubriquet! Do adjust the ingredients to your liking. These kebabs can also be made into sausage shapes.*

1. Mix together the minced meat, onion, mango powder, green chillies and pomegranate. Purée in a blender or food processor until smooth then remove and place on a plate.
2. In a microwave-safe flat dish, place 2 teaspoons of ghee and heat at full power, uncovered, for 1 minute. Break the eggs into the ghee and scramble lightly. Cook, uncovered, for another minute.
3. Add the soft eggs to the meat mixture then stir in the cornflour, salt and garam masala. Divide the mixture into eight portions and pat each one into a flat saucer shape, thicker in the middle and thin around the edges.
4. Grease the surface of a 25 cm/10 inch browning skillet with ghee. Place the kebabs on it and cook, uncovered, at full power for 8 minutes, turning over halfway through. Adjust the cooking time to obtain the desired results, especially if your skillet is smaller and you have to cook in batches. When cooked, the chhappars should be crisp at the edges but still soft in the middle. Stand for 2 minutes then serve with a sour chutney and salad.

**Serves 4**

450 g/1 lb minced beef or
  mutton
1 large onion, chopped
2 teaspoons green mango
  powder (aamchoor)
4 green chillies, chopped
1 tablespoon dried
  pomegranate seeds
2 eggs
2 teaspoons ghee, plus extra
  for greasing
50 g/2 oz/½ cup cornflour
salt, to taste
2 teaspoons garam masala

**Prep 10 min
Cooking 10 min
+ standing time 2 min**

# Premi Kabaab Phaankein

SLICES OF MEATY ROMANCE

**Serves 4**

450 g/1 lb lean lamb, finely
  minced
1 small onion, finely chopped
1 tablespoon grated root
  ginger
4 cloves garlic, crushed
2 green chillies, finely
  chopped
2 teaspoons salt, or to taste
2 teaspoons garam masala
pinch of bicarbonate of soda
2 tablespoons finely chopped
  coriander leaves
1 tablespoon cooking oil
2 egg whites
2 tablespoons finely slivered
  almonds and pistachios
lettuce, onion rings and
  tomato slices, to garnish
yoghurt sauce or chutney,
  to serve

**Prep** 10 min
**Cooking** 8 min
+ standing time 5 min

*You can make this romantic savoury lamb cake in virtually no time at all; it requires hardly any effort or expertise. A loaf of bread beneath the bough, a flask of chilled wine and a few of these slices are all that two lovers need to have their own private party!*

1. Mix the lamb, onion, ginger, garlic, chillies, salt, garam masala, bicarbonate of soda and coriander leaves in a bowl and blend well.
2. Grease the base and sides of a 25cm/10 inch microwave-proof pie dish or skillet with oil. Pour the meat mixture into it and pat down.
3. Whisk the egg whites until frothy and spread them on top of the meat mixture. Scatter with almonds and pistachios.
4. Cook, uncovered, at full power for 8 minutes, or until the meat is cooked (to test, insert a cocktail stick in the middle of the cake: it should come out clean).
5. Remove the dish from the oven and let it stand for 5 minutes. Then, running a sharp knife around the dish, transfer the cake on to a serving platter and slice. Serve on a bed of lettuce, surrounded by onion and tomato slices, accompanied by a yoghurt sauce or chutney.

# Malaai Kofta Khazaana

### FRESHLY MINTED LAMB MEATBALLS

*This must be the simplest non-vegetarian kofta curry ever. While cooking, the meatballs release their own juices, enriching the sauce the koftas swim in. If desired, more chillies and spices can be added in the second stage of cooking.*

1. Place the lamb in a bowl, add ½ teaspoon of salt and the garlic and mix thoroughly. Divide the mixture into 8 or 12 portions and roll each one into a ball.

2. In a microwave-safe casserole of 1.8 litre/3 pint/7½ cup capacity, stir the ready gravy and cream together with additional salt to taste. Cook, half-covered, at full power for 5 minutes, or until the gravy begins to bubble. Drop in the meatballs and continue to cook at full power for 10 minutes, or until the koftas are cooked through.

3. Remove from the oven, stir in the garam masala and mint, fully cover with the lid and let the dish stand for 5 minutes. Serve with a rice or bread dish.

**Serves 4**

225 g/8 oz minced lamb
salt, to taste
2 cloves garlic, crushed
300 ml/½ pint/1¼ cups
 meat ready gravy
 (see p.36)
2 tablespoons double cream
1 teaspoon garam masala
1 tablespoon chopped mint
 leaves

**Prep 10 min**
**Cooking 15 min**
**+ standing time 5 min**

# Bhuni Maans Botiyaan

BBQ LAMB CHOPS

**Serves 4**

4 thick lamb chops, about
   450 g/1 lb in total
2 tablespoons malt vinegar
4 tablespoons/⅓ cup pure
   orange juice
2 tablespoons chopped onion
2 cloves garlic
½ teaspoon turmeric powder
4 green chillies, shredded
2 teaspoons red chilli powder
1 tablespoon mustard seeds
1 teaspoon garam masala
1 teaspoon salt, or to taste
2 tablespoons ghee
twists of lemon slices,
   to garnish
chopped coriander leaves,
   to garnish

**Prep 10 min
+ marinating time
Cooking 18 min
+ standing time 2 min**

*These delicious sizzlers come out a treat in the microwave. This recipe is on the hot side so do adjust the chilli and spice content of the paste to your liking. You can similarly barbecue pork chops or make sweet and sour lamb or pork chops by adding 1 tablespoon of brown sugar and 1 tablespoon of tomato ketchup. You can replace the vinegar and orange juice with 6 tablespoons of plain yoghurt, if preferred.*

1. With a sharp knife, score the chops on both sides. Pour in the vinegar and orange juice over the chops, making sure the liquid soaks on both sides. Leave to marinate overnight.
2. Grind the onion, garlic, turmeric, chillies, chilli powder, mustard seeds, garam masala and salt together to make a paste. Smear it generously over both sides of the chops and leave for a couple of hours to marinate.
3. Use half the ghee to grease the base of a 25cm/10-inch browning skillet and heat, covered, at full power for 2 minutes.
4. Place the chops in the hot ghee, return to the microwave and cook, covered, on high for 8 minutes.
5. Uncover, turn over the chops, add the remaining ghee, replace the lid and continue to cook on high for another 8 minutes, or until the chops are cooked through.
6. Remove from the oven and let the dish stand, fully covered, for 2 minutes to allow completion of the cooking process. Serve garnished with the lemon and coriander, accompanied by a sauce and/or vegetables of your choice.

# Shikaar Vindaloo

PORK IN SPICY SAUCE

*This dish is an offering from South India, where*
*even the mild curries are hotter than the hot ones*
*of the North. A vindaloo is usually hot and sour.*
*Mustard oil, vinegar, tamarind juice and desiccated*
*coconut are always used in its preparation. Adjust*
*the quantity of these ingredients to suit your palate*
*or serve with a cooling raita. A similar vindaloo can*
*be made with duck.*

1. Pierce the diced pork all over with a fork then combine in a
bowl with the vinegar and leave to marinate for 2 hours. Stir
once during this period and make sure that all sides of the
meat have soaked in the vinegar.

2. In a microwave-compatible casserole of 1.8 litre/3 pint/7½
cup capacity, place the oil, onion and garlic and cook,
uncovered, at full power for 3 minutes. Stir in the vindaloo
powder and continue to cook at full power for 1 more minute.

3. Toss in the pork and green chillies and blend thoroughly,
then pour in the measured water and salt. Cover and cook
on high for 12 minutes, or until the pork is fork-tender.

4. Remove the lid, add the tamarind juice, cover and cook on
high for another 5 minutes.

5. Remove the dish from the oven, sprinkle with the coconut,
replace the cover tightly and leave to stand for 5 minutes.
Stir before serving.

Serves 4

450 g/1 lb lean pork, diced
4 tablespoons/⅓ cup cider
  vinegar
2 tablespoons mustard oil
1 large onion, finely chopped
4 cloves garlic, chopped
1 tablespoon vindaloo
  powder (see p.30)
2 green chillies, chopped
150 ml /¼ pint/⅔ cup warm
  water
2 teaspoons salt, or to taste
2 tablespoons tamarind juice,
  fresh or canned
2 tablespoons desiccated
  coconut

Prep 10 min
+ marinating time
Cooking 21 min
+ standing time 5 min

# Bhoona Gosht

BRAISED MEAT MADRAS

Serves 4

450 g/1 lb lean beef, diced
4 tablespoons/⅓ cup cider
  vinegar
2 tablespoons mustard oil
1 large onion, finely chopped
4 cloves garlic, crushed
4 green chillies, sliced
  lengthways
1 tablespoon red chilli
  powder
2 teaspoons garam masala
2 teaspoons salt, or to taste
2 tomatoes, chopped
2 tablespoons desiccated
  coconut

Prep 10 min
+ marinating time
Cooking 20 min
+ standing time 5 min

*This is a really hot number from the southern shores of India. Do feel free to adjust the quantity of chilli and garlic to suit your palate. You can use an alternative oil, should you so choose.*

1. Pierce the beef dice all over with a fork. Spoon the vinegar over the beef, making sure no part of the meat is untouched by vinegar. Set aside for 2 hours to marinate.
2. Place the oil, onion and garlic in a microwave-safe covered dish of 1.8 litre/3 pint/7½ cup capacity and cook, uncovered, at full power for 3 minutes. Add the green chilli, chilli powder and garam masala, blend and microwave on high for 1 minute.
3. Stir in the beef, salt and tomatoes. Cover the dish and cook at full power for 16 minutes, or until the beef pieces are springy. Stir a couple of times during cooking and add splashes of water if the meat appears too dry. (If you want the meat to be softer, cook it a little longer.)
4. When cooked, remove the dish from the microwave and leave to stand, fully covered, for 5 minutes. Sprinkle with the coconut and serve.

# Keema Andaa

## Egg and Mincemeat

*This is an ideal quick-and-easy curry that can be served with rice or bread. Any meat can be used, as long as it is lean and finely minced.*

1. In a microwave-proof casserole of 2.4 litre/4 pint/10 cup capacity, place the oil and onion and cook, without covering, at full power for 3 minutes.
2. Stir in the turmeric, chilli powder, lamb and ginger one by one, blending thoroughly. Add the yoghurt, salt and measured water and stir well. Cover and cook at full power for 8 minutes.
3. Take the dish out of the microwave and carefully remove the lid. Add the peas, eggs and tomatoes. Replace the lid, return to the microwave and cook at full power for another 8 minutes, or until the meat is cooked through.
4. Remove from the oven, uncover, sprinkle with the garam masala and coriander. Cover with the lid and leave to stand for 5 minutes. Stir before serving.

Serves 4

2 teaspoons cooking oil
1 large onion, finely chopped
1 teaspoon turmeric powder
1 teaspoon red chilli powder
450 g/1 lb lean lamb mince
1 teaspoon grated root ginger
150 ml/¼ pint/⅔ cup plain yoghurt
salt, to taste
300 ml/½ pint/1¼ cups warm water
75 g/3 oz/½ cup shelled green peas
4 hard-boiled eggs, shelled and halved
2 tomatoes, chopped
2 teaspoons garam masala
2 tablespoons chopped coriander leaves

Prep 10 min
Cooking 19 min
+ standing time 5 min

# Pasinda Tikka Do-Piazza

MUTTON PIECES IN ONION SAUCE

Serves 4

450 g/1 lb boneless mutton
600 ml/1 pint/2½ cups plain
  yogurt, whisked
100 g/4 oz/½ cup ghee
450 g/1 lb onions, sliced
4 cloves
1 teaspoon red chilli powder
2.5 cm/1 inch cinnamon stick,
  broken
4 green cardamoms, cracked
2 bay leaves
salt, to taste
2 teaspoons poppy seeds,
  crushed
1 tablespoon flaked almonds
pinch of saffron strands

Prep 15 min
+ marinating time
Cooking 30 min
+ standing time 5 min

*Do-piazza ('double the onion') is an offering from the Punjab region. There are various schools of thought about the onion content in this type of dish, but the sum and substance is that the dish contains a lot of onion. This is a mild and moist dish, and is made with boneless meat (use mutton, lamb, pork or chicken). I have devised this Punjabi recipe to be cooked in a Kashmiri way. Serve as a side dish with a main meal, as a tea-time snack or with drinks.*

1. Beat the mutton with a kitchen mallet and cut it into 2.5 cm / 1 inch cubes. Place the cubes on a wooden board, prick them with a fork. Take a quarter of the yoghurt, smear it over the mutton pieces and leave to marinate for 1 hour.
2. Place the ghee and onion in a microwave-safe casserole of 2.4 litre/4 pint/10 cup capacity. Cook, uncovered, at full power for 5 minutes, or until the onion changes colour. Stir halfway through cooking.
3. Add the mutton, cloves, chilli powder, cinnamon, cardamom, bay leaves and the remaining yoghurt and cook, covered, at full power for 20 minutes, or until the meat is tender.
4. Take the casserole out of the oven and add the salt, poppy seeds and almonds. Replace the lid, return to the oven and continue cooking on high for another 5 minutes, or until most of the liquid has soaked into the meat and the mixture is moist.
5. Scatter the saffron strands over the meat and leave to stand, covered, for 5 minutes before serving.

# Roghan Josh

VEAL IN SPICY SAUCE

*Roghan josh means that the dish should look roghani (glittering red – from the spices and cooking oil) and offer josh (inspiration). Given that it was the Mughal chefs who perfected this dish, roghan josh can rightly be regarded as the Mughal legacy to Indian cuisine. It can also be made with lamb or mutton but not pork. Cooking this dish in a microwave saves time and gives the preparation a succulent, flavoursome, superlative taste.*

1. Prick the veal pieces all over with a fork. Add the yoghurt and stir thoroughly. Leave to marinate for 1 hour.
2. Place the oil, onion and garlic in a microwave-safe casserole of 2.4 litre/4 pint/10 cup capacity. Cook, uncovered, at full power for 3 minutes. Stir in the turmeric, ground coriander, salt, cardamoms, chilli powder and the veal, together with the yoghurt it was marinating in. Stir well, cover with the lid and cook at full power for 12 minutes, stirring once.
3. Add the ready gravy, mix and cook, covered, at full power for another 10 minutes, or until the meat is cooked through and tender and the sauce is well blended.
4. Remove from the oven and stir in the garam masala. Replace the lid tightly and leave to stand for 5 minutes. Stir and serve, to be truly inspired!

Serves 4

450 g/1 lb veal, diced
6 tablespoons/½ cup plain yoghurt
3 tablespoons cooking oil
1 medium onion, chopped
2 cloves garlic, crushed
½ teaspoon turmeric powder
1 teaspoon ground coriander
1 teaspoon salt, or to taste
4 green cardamoms, cracked
½ teaspoon red chilli powder
600 ml/1 pint/2½ cups meat ready gravy (see p.36)
1 teaspoon garam masala

Prep 10 min
+ marinating time
Cooking 25 min
+ standing time 5 min

# Gosht Jhalfrezi

BEEF À LA FRASER

Serves 4

2 large onions, finely
  chopped
25 g/1 oz/¼ cup blanched
  almonds
1 tablespoon chopped root
  ginger
salt, to taste
1 tablespoon coriander seeds
1 teaspoon black cumin
  seeds
4 cloves
1 brown cardamom, cracked
4 black peppercorns
450 g/1 lb beef chuck steak
2 tablespoons ghee
2 bay leaves
150 ml/¼ pint/⅔ cup plain
  yoghurt
4 green cardamoms, cracked
1 teaspoon red chilli powder
1 teaspoon turmeric powder
150 ml/¼ pint/⅔ cup double
  cream
½ teaspoon saffron strands
1 teaspoon garam masala
150 ml/¼ pint/⅔ cup warm
  water

Prep 10 min
+ marinating time
Cooking 35 min
+ standing time 5 min

*Jhalfrezi is not the name of a particular dish, nor is it a method of cooking. In fact, it is not dissimilar to the Mog cuisine, prevalent during the Raj in the Assam/Tripura regions of India. In this case, during the Raj, a British officer of the catering corps, Lt Colonel Tom Fraser, was stationed at Calcutta. Realizing how hot and spicy some of the Indian dishes were, Fraser exercised his influence to get these dishes mellowed and moderated.  Hence the dishes cooked under Fraser's influence came to be variously predicated by the Indian cooks as 'Farezi', 'Frezi' or 'Pharesi'. 'Jhaal' in Bengali is water or liquid. Thus any curried dishes of this ilk were christened 'jhalfrezi'.*

1. Mix half the onion together with the almonds, ginger, salt, coriander seeds, cumin seeds, cloves, brown cardamom and black peppercorns and grind to a smooth paste. Set aside.
2. Cut the beef into 2.5cm/1 inch cubes and prick them all over with a fork. Coat liberally with the prepared paste and leave to marinate for at least 2 hours.
3. Place the ghee, the remaining onion and the bay leaves in a microwave-friendly casserole of  2.4 litre/4 pint/10 cup capacity. Cook, uncovered, at full power for 3 minutes, then remove half of the cooked onion and set aside.
4. Add the yoghurt, green cardamoms, chilli and turmeric powders to the onion mixture in the casserole, stir thoroughly and cook, half-covered, at full power for another 2 minutes.
5. Pile in the marinated meat, stir and cook, covered, at full power for 10 minutes, stirring once halfway through.
6. Beat the cream together with the saffron and add to the meat mixture with the garam masala and the reserved fried onions. Pour in the water, half-cover with the lid, and cook on high for 20 minutes, or until the beef is tender, stirring once or twice during cooking.
7. Remove from the oven and leave to stand, tightly covered, for 5 minutes. Stir before serving.

# Murgh Musallam

GLAZED POUSSIN

By tradition, this dish is cooked by the live fire and smoke of a tandoor (clay oven). However, the chicken comes out moist and gloriously succulent when cooked in a microwave. Given that the marinade is fat-free, the finished dish is a veritable delight for calorie-conscious weight-watchers. What it lacks in microwave-cooking is the scorched, reddish-orange colour of tandoori cooking. The answer is: either use a browning skillet or glaze the chicken with a mixture of honey and tandoori masala, or simply a combination of food colouring and paprika.

1. Pick over and wash the rice then leave it to soak for an hour or so. Drain and set aside.
2. Place the poussin on a platter. Wrapping a piece of clean cloth around your fingers, remove the skin. Wash and dry the poussin then prick it all over with a fork and, using a sharp knife, make several gashes in the bird.
3. Mix the honey and tandoori powder into a paste and brush it all over the chicken, including into the gashes and cavity.
4. Prepare the marinade by grinding together the chopped onion, garlic, ginger, peppercorns, garam masala, poppy seeds and half the yoghurt. Rub this paste evenly all over the chicken, including the gashes and cavity. Leave to marinate at room temperature (or in the refrigerator) for 2 hours.
5. In a microwave-safe dish, place half the ghee with the drained rice and cook, uncovered, at full power for 2 minutes. Stir in the salt, chilli powder, asafoetida, almonds, chironji nuts or raisins, khoya and half the water and cook, half-covered, at full power for 4 minutes.
6. Place the poussin on a microwave-proof meat roasting rack, breast downwards. Cover loosely with greaseproof paper and cook at full power for 3 minutes. Turn the bird breast-side up and continue cooking for another 3 minutes. Remove from the oven.
7. Remove the paper and stuff the rice mixture into the chicken cavity. Secure with a thread to prevent spillage. Place the bird

Serves 4

50 g/2 oz basmati rice
1 poussin (baby chicken), about 450 g/1 lb
2 tablespoons clear honey
1 tablespoon tandoori powder (see p.29)
1 large onion, chopped
4 cloves garlic, chopped
1 tablespoon grated root ginger
4 black peppercorns
1 teaspoon garam masala
1 teaspoon poppy seeds
150 ml/¼ pint/⅔ cup plain yoghurt
2 tablespoons ghee or olive oil
salt, to taste
1 teaspoon red chilli powder
pinch of asafoetida powder
1 tablespoon flaked almonds
2 teaspoons chironji nuts, or raisins
50 g/2 oz khoya (see p.37)
300 ml/½ pint/1¼ cups warm water
½ teaspoon saffron strands

Prep 15 min
+ soaking and marinating times
Cooking 18 min
+ standing time 5 min

over the remaining ghee in a microwave-safe dish, add the remaining water and yoghurt together with any liquid left from the stuffing mixture. Cover and cook on high for 6 minutes, or until the liquid is absorbed and the meat tender. Keep checking as cooking times will vary.

8. Remove the poussin from the microwave. Sprinkle it with the saffron strands, cover and leave to stand for 5 minutes. Remove and discard the thread before serving.

# Murgh Makkhani

## BUTTER CHICKEN

*The sauce is the main ingredient of this dish. If you have any leftover cooked chicken, duck or other meat in the refrigerator, you can simply prepare the buttery sauce to serve with it.*

1. Prick the chicken pieces all over with a fork. Smear the yoghurt all around them and leave to soak for an hour or so. Wash off the yoghurt, dry the chicken and set aside.

2. In a microwave-compatible casserole of 1.8 litre/3 pint/7½ cup capacity, place the butter, cream and chicken. Cover and cook at full power for 6 minutes, stirring halfway through.

3. In another suitable casserole, place the onion, garlic, ginger, pepper, chilli powder, measured water, tomato purée and salt and cook, half-covered, on high for 6 minutes. Stir a couple of times during cooking.

4. Pour the onion mixture into the casserole containing the chicken. Cover and cook at full power for 5 minutes, or until the chicken is tender and the sauce is fully blended. Stir once during cooking.

5. Remove the casserole from the oven, uncover and sprinkle with the garam masala and coriander leaves. Replace the lid and leave to stand for 5 minutes before serving.

**Serves 4**

450 g/1 lb boneless chicken, diced
4 tablespoons/⅓ cup plain yoghurt
100 g/4 oz/½ cup unsalted butter
4 tablespoons/⅓ cup double cream
1 small onion, ground
4 cloves garlic, ground
1 tablespoon grated root ginger
pinch of ground black pepper
1 teaspoon red chilli powder
150 ml/¼ pint/⅔ cup lukewarm water
2 tablespoons tomato purée
salt, to taste
2 teaspoons garam masala
2 tablespoons chopped coriander leaves

**Prep 15 min**
**+ marinating time**
**Cooking 17 min**
**+ standing time 5 min**

# Shaahi Murgh Quorma

ROYAL CHICKEN KORMA

**Serves 4**

450 g/1 lb chicken breast
  fillets, skinned
4 tablespoons/¹/₃ cup plain
  yoghurt
4 tablespoons/¹/₃ cup ghee
2 medium onions, finely
  chopped
4 cloves garlic, crushed
1 teaspoon grated root ginger
2 teaspoons garam masala
4 tablespoons tomato purée
½ teaspoon red chilli
  powder
3 tablespoons/¼ cup double
  cream
½ teaspoon green
  cardamom powder
150 ml/¼ pint/⅔ cup
  lukewarm water
1 teaspoon lemon juice
salt, to taste
½ teaspoon freshly ground
  black pepper

**Prep 10 min**
**+ marinating time**
**Cooking 18 min**
**+ standing time 2 min**

*Quorma is similar to other meat dishes, except that this one, when ready, is mild and has no gravy – just thick and rich moisture after the liquid has evaporated. For variety, add ½ teaspoon saffron strands, steeped in milk or hot water, just before serving. Now you have a quorma dish which will be the envy of the royal dining halls!*

1. Dice the chicken and prick the pieces with a fork. Rub the yoghurt all over them and leave to marinate for 1 hour.
2. Place half the ghee in a microwave-proof casserole and heat, covered, at full power for 2 minutes. Add diced chicken together with the marinade liquid and stir well. Replace the lid and cook on high for 4 minutes, stirring once halfway through cooking. Remove the casserole from the oven, transfer the contents to a covered bowl and set aside.
3. Add the remaining ghee to the cooking dish and stir in the onions, garlic, ginger, garam masala, tomato purée and chilli powder. Cook, uncovered, at full power for 5 minutes, stirring occasionally.
4. Take the dish out of the oven. Add the reserved chicken, including any juices it has exuded, and all the remaining ingredients. Mix well then cover, return to the microwave and cook on high for another 7 minutes, or until the chicken is cooked through and the liquid has almost evaporated.
5. Remove from the oven, stir carefully (if using saffron, add it now) and leave, covered, to stand for 2 minutes. Uncover and serve the royalty – your dinner guests!

# Dhansak

## CHICKEN WITH VEGE-LENTILS

*This is the original dhansak recipe, a speciality of the Indian Parsees (people of Persian-Iranian extraction). The dish cooks very well in the microwave and produces a smooth, creamy sauce for the chicken. It is usually served with boiled rice. The chicken can be substituted with mutton, lamb or duck (with all fat trimmed off) and you can vary the choice of lentils. The virtually fat-free nature of the dish makes it even more attractive.*

1. Pick over and wash the lentils then leave to soak for 2 hours. Drain and set aside.
2. In a microwave-safe lidded casserole of 3 litre/5 pint/12½ cup capacity, place the ghee, onion and garlic and cook, uncovered, at full power for 3 minutes.
3. Add the drained lentils plus all the remaining ingredients, except the coriander leaves. Cover and cook at full power for 25 minutes.
4. Remove the casserole from the oven, take out the chicken pieces and set aside. Put the vegetable-lentil mixture in a blender or food processor and purée.
5. Return the purée and chicken pieces to the casserole and cook, covered, on high for another 5 minutes, or until the chicken is tender and the sauce is well combined.
6. Take the casserole out of the oven and leave, covered, to stand for 5 minutes. Scatter with the coriander leaves before serving.

Serves 4

225 g/8 oz/1 cup mixed lentils (toor, masoor, urad)
1 tablespoon ghee
1 large onion, finely chopped
2 cloves garlic, chopped
1 tablespoon grated root ginger
1 teaspoon turmeric powder
2 teaspoons garam masala
1 teaspoon red chilli powder
1 teaspoon lemon juice
1 aubergine/eggplant , cut in chunks
4 tomatoes, chopped
2 potatoes, chopped
225 g/8 oz/2 cups pumpkin (kaddu), cut in chunks
2 green chillies, seeded and chopped
900 g/2 lb chicken, skinned and jointed
900 ml/1½ pints/3¾ cups lukewarm water
2 teaspoons salt, or to taste
2 tablespoons chopped coriander leaves

Prep 15 min
+ soaking time
Cooking 33 min
+ standing time 5 min

# Hari Battakh Rasedaar

## CURRIED GREEN DUCK

**Serves 4**

450 g/1 lb duck, ready weight
2 teaspoons lime juice
1 teaspoon salt, or to taste
leaves and tender stems of a
   large bunch of coriander
2 large green peppers, cored
4 green chillies, or to taste
300 ml/½ pint/1¼ cups
   meat ready gravy
   (see p.36)
water, as necessary
1 teaspoon garam masala

Prep 15 min
+ marinating time
Cooking 15 min
+ standing time 5 min

*Duck is rich and juicy and is often used in Indian dishes. The meat is full of natural oils, so when substituting duck for other meat, go easy on the cooking oil or ghee! This dish is easy to cook in the microwave, as it is nouvelle cuisine, so to speak. Cook it for your family and friends and earn full marks for taste and novelty value.*

1. Skin the duck, trim off any visible fat and cut into small pieces. Prick with a fork. Combine the lime juice with a large pinch of salt and rub over the duck. Leave to marinate for 1 hour.
2. Meanwhile, reserve some of the coriander to use as a garnish then grind the remainder to a paste with the green peppers and chillies. After the duck has been marinating for an hour, smear the pieces thickly with the paste.
3. Arrange the duck pieces in a casserole of 2.4 litre/4 pint/10 cup capacity and pour the ready gravy over them. The duck pieces should be fully submerged in liquid; use additional water if necessary. Add extra salt as needed. Cover and cook at full power for 15 minutes, or until the duck is fully cooked.
4. Remove the casserole from the oven. There may be a layer of oil (released by the duck) on the surface. Keep it if you like, or remove it and save for cooking other dishes. Stir in the garam masala and scatter the coriander leaves (whole or chopped) over the preparation. Replace the lid firmly and leave to stand for 5 minutes. Stir before serving.

# Doodhiya Khargosh Masaaledaar

DEVILLED MILKY RABBIT

*This is another easy dish which anyone can try. If you are cooking for larger numbers, use a hare, which is bigger than rabbit. Rabbit releases natural juices, so adjust the amount of added liquid to suit. As always, adapt the spices to your liking.*

1. Prick the rabbit all over with a fork. Combine the lemon juice with a pinch of salt and rub this mixture all over the rabbit. Leave to marinate for 1 hour. (Alternatively, leave the rabbit pieces to soak in salted water for 2 hours, then drain off the water.)

2. In a microwave-proof casserole of 2.4 litre/4 pint/10 cup capacity, place the ghee, onion, garlic and ginger and cook, uncovered, at full power for 2 minutes. Add the bay leaves, cardamom, cinnamon, turmeric, ground coriander, garam masala, chilli powder, tomato purée and yoghurt and stir well. Continue cooking, covered, on high for another 3 minutes.

3. Add the rabbit, milk and salt to taste. Cover and cook at full power for 18 minutes, or until the rabbit is tender and most
of the liquid has evaporated, or is reduced to the desired consistency.

4. Remove the casserole from the oven, stir in the coriander leaves and put the lid back on. Leave to stand for 5 minutes. Stir before serving with a rice or bread dish, and the usual other accompaniments.

Serves 4

900 g/2 lb rabbit, skinned and jointed
1 tablespoon lemon juice
salt, as required
1 tablespoon ghee
1 large onion, ground
2 cloves garlic, ground
2.5 cm/1 inch piece root ginger, ground
2 bay leaves
1 brown cardamom, cracked
2 cinnamon sticks, 2.5 cm/1 inch long
1 teaspoon turmeric powder
1 teaspoon ground coriander
2 teaspoons garam masala
1 teaspoon red chilli powder
2 tablespoons tomato purée
2 tablespoons plain yoghurt
300 ml/½ pint/1¼ cups milk
2 tablespoons chopped coriander leaves

Prep 15 min
+ marinating time
Cooking 23 min
+ standing time 5 min

# Teetar Dumpukht

## PARTRIDGE IN CREAM SAUCE

**Serves 4**

4 partridges
100 g/4 oz/1 cup gram flour
  (besan)
2 large onions, minced
1 teaspoon ground cinnamon
2.5 cm/1 inch piece root
  ginger, ground
2 ripe pears, peeled, cored
  and mashed
1 tablespoon unsalted butter
2 cloves garlic, sliced
2 cloves, crushed
1 bay leaf
1 teaspoon garam masala
pinch of ground nutmeg
1 tablespoon lemon juice
300 ml/½ pint/1¼ cups meat
  ready gravy (see p.36)
salt, to taste
4 blanched almonds, ground
6 tablespoons double cream
½ teaspoon green
  cardamom powder
½ teaspoon saffron strands

**Prep 15 min**
**+ marinating time**
**Cooking 21 min**
**+ standing time 5 min**

*Partridge and pears, when steamed in the microwave in a thick, creamy sauce, taste absolutely fabulous. Don't wait for Christmas; offer this dish to your true love at any time of year! You can make a similar preparation with quail (bateir).*

1. Cut the partridges in half all the way down the back. Clean, rinse and pat dry. Rub the gram flour all over the partridge pieces and leave for 30 minutes. Then wash off the flour and pat dry.

2. Combine the minced onions, cinnamon, ginger and pears, thickly smear this mixture over the partridges and set aside.

3. In a microwave-compatible casserole of 1.8 litre/3 pint/7½ cup capacity, place the butter, garlic, cloves, bay leaf, garam masala and nutmeg and cook, uncovered, at full power for 2 minutes, stirring halfway through.

4. Add the partridge pieces and their marinade to the casserole and continue to cook on high for another 4 minutes. Turn over the partridge pieces a couple of times during cooking so that they are well coated with the mixture and receive heat on all sides.

5. Stir in the lemon juice, ready gravy and add salt to taste. Cover tightly with the lid and cook at full power for 15 minutes. Halfway through cooking, stir in the almonds and cream. Cover and complete the cooking period, continuing until the partridge meat is tender and the gravy is reduced to the required consistency (most of the liquid should evaporate).

6. Remove the casserole from the oven and add the cardamom powder and saffron strands. Replace the lid quickly and leave to stand for 5 minutes. Stir before serving.

# Khat-Mitthi Jheenga Malaai

## SWEET-AND-SOUR YOGHURT PRAWNS

*People from Bengal and Goa make this dish with great relish, the Goan version being hotter (so adjust the chilli and spice content as necessary). Those requiring a creamy finish should substitute cream for the water. Either way, it is a finger-licking dish!*

1. In a microwave-proof casserole of 1.8 litre/3 pint/7½ cup capacity, place the oil, ginger, green chilli, cloves, cardamom pods, bay leaves, cumin seeds, turmeric powder and red chilli powder. Stir well and cook, without cover, at full power for 1 minute. Then stir in the salt, sugar and yoghurt and continue to cook, half-covered, for a further 2 minutes.
2. Stir in the prawns and mix thoroughly. Pour in the water, cover and cook at full power for 7 minutes, or until the prawns are cooked and the sauce is thick (watch out for the evaporation of water: stop when desired).
3. Remove the casserole from the oven and sprinkle with the garam masala and caramelized onions. Replace the lid and leave to stand for 5 minutes, then uncover, stir and serve.

Serves 4

1 tablespoon cooking oil
1 tablespoon grated root
   ginger
1 green chilli, chopped
2 cloves
2 green cardamom pods,
   cracked
2 bay leaves
½ teaspoon black cumin
   seeds, or 1 teaspoon white
   ones
½ teaspoon turmeric powder
½ teaspoon red chilli
   powder
salt, to taste
2 teaspoons sugar
2 tablespoons plain yoghurt,
   or 1 teaspoon lemon juice
450 g/1 lb prawns, peeled and
   deveined
150 ml/¼ pint/⅔ cup
   lukewarm water
pinch of garam masala
1 tablespoon caramelized
   onions (see p.32)

Prep 10 min
Cooking 10 min
+ standing time 5 min

# Dum Machhli Phaankein

## STEAMED COD FILLETS

**Serves 4**

8 cod fillet steaks (about
   450 g/1 lb), skinned and any
   bones removed
salt, as required
1 tablespoon lemon juice
1 tablespoon mustard seeds
2 cloves garlic
2 green chillies
1 teaspoon grated fresh root
   ginger
1 tablespoon coriander
   leaves
½ teaspoon turmeric powder

Prep 5 min
+ marinating time
Cooking 5 min
+ standing time 2 min

*The microwave oven seems to be the ideal medium for cooking this fish dish. If more convenient, you may use the fillets of a smaller fish, haddock. By tradition, these fillet-rolls are wrapped in banana leaves but you may use baking foil. As a last resort, just fold the fillets in a pinwheel (Catherine wheel) fashion and secure with cocktail sticks. You may also stuff a filling of your choice into these rolls.*

1. Place the fish fillets on a platter. Combine 1 teaspoon of salt and the lemon juice and rub this mixture over the fillets on both sides. Leave to rest.
2. Grind all the remaining ingredients into a paste, adding more salt if desired. Rub this mixture all over the fillets then roll each fillet into a wheel and wrap or secure as described above.
3. In a microwave-proof shallow covered dish, arrange the spiced fish rolls. Cover and cook at full power for 5 minutes, turning over the rolls halfway through cooking. Be careful not to overcook: when done the fish should be turning translucent and still moist.
4. Remove from the oven and leave to stand, covered, for 2 minutes. Serve with a salad, sauce or chutney of your choice.

# Jheenga Lahsuni

## GARLIC PRAWNS

*If you like garlic, you will love this recipe – adjust the amount included to your liking. For variety, you may highlight the tomato sauce or chilli powder. There is fair scope for experimentation.*

1. Wash and dry the prawns. Combine the lemon juice with a pinch of salt, rub this mixture over the prawns and let them rest.
2. Chop off the green sections of the spring onions and shred them. Set aside to use as a garnish. Chop the white parts of the spring onions.
3. In a microwave-proof covered dish, place the butter with the white parts of the spring onions and add the garlic, ginger and chilli. Cook, uncovered, at full power for 3 minutes, stirring once halfway through.
4. Add the prawns, cornflour and soya sauce, together with additional salt to taste, and stir thoroughly. Cover, return to the microwave and cook at full power for 5 minutes, or until the prawns turn pink and are cooked. Stir once or twice during this cooking period.
5. Remove the dish from the oven and leave to stand for 2 minutes. Garnish with the reserved spring onions and serve.

Serves 4

450 g/1 lb prawns/shrimp, peeled and deveined
1 tablespoon lemon juice
salt, as required
4 spring onions
1 tablespoon butter
6 cloves garlic, sliced
1 teaspoon grated root ginger
1 green chilli, shredded
1 tablespoon cornflour
1 tablespoon soya sauce

Prep 10 min
+ resting time
Cooking 8 min
+ standing time 2 min

# Kekda Malaaidaar

CRAB AND COCONUT CREAM

Serves 4

1 tablespoon ghee
1 medium onion, chopped
2 cloves garlic, chopped
½ teaspoon grated root
  ginger
2 green chillies, chopped
1 teaspoon chopped curry
  leaves
4 crabs, boiled, shelled and
  flaked
salt, to taste
150 ml/¼ pint/⅔ cup coconut
  milk
½ teaspoon red chilli
  powder
1 tablespoon desiccated
  coconut
1 tablespoon chopped
  coriander leaves

Prep 10 min
+ boiling of crabs
Cooking 10 min
+ standing time 5 min

*This dish is a godsend for seafood lovers. The taste is sweet (a combination of onion and coconut) and yet leaves a warm glow in the mouth (chillies!). Adjust these components to your taste. Serve the preparation with a rice or bread dish. If you make the liquid thinner, you will have a healthy soup!*

1. In a microwave-safe lidded dish of 1.2 litre/2 pint/5 cup capacity, place the ghee, onion, garlic, ginger, green chillies and curry leaves and cook, uncovered, at full power for 3 minutes, stirring once.
2. Add the crab meat, salt and stir. Pour in the coconut milk and chilli powder and cook, uncovered, at full power for 7 minutes, or until the liquid has blended with the crab meat. Stir once or twice during cooking.
3. Remove the dish from the oven, sprinkle with the coconut, cover and leave to stand for 5 minutes. Stir, garnish with the coriander leaves and serve.

# Shaark (Haangur) Machhli Shaandaar

SHARK IN RED SEA

*The riparian people of India – from the eastern and western seaboards – are very fond of fish dishes. This one, being a southern dish, has a preponderance of coconut and chilli. Shark has a subtle flavour and, when bobbing in a red chilli sauce, it has more bite! Experiment with salmon and make your own variety of pink salmon!*

1. Combine the minced onion, garlic, ginger and green chilli in a bowl. Remove half of the mixture and reserve. To the rest, add the lemon juice and make a paste. Coat the shark fillets all over with this paste and leave to marinate for 30 minutes, or longer.

2. In a microwave-compatible casserole of 1.8 litre/3 pint/7½ cup capacity, place half the oil and heat it, uncovered, at full power for 2 minutes. Arrange the shark fillets over the oil and cook, uncovered, at full power for 2 minutes, turning over the fillets halfway through. The fillets are done when they lose their raw look and turn bright. Drain and transfer the fillets on to a plate.

3. Add the rest of the oil to the cooking dish together with the reserved herb mixture. Add the turmeric, ground coriander, fennel powder, chilli powder, paprika, tomato purée and salt and blend thoroughly. Cook, half-covered, on high for 5 minutes, stirring occasionally. Pour in the coconut milk and continue to cook at full power for a further 3 minutes, or until the sauce is on the boil.

4. Carefully drop the shark fillets, together with any released juices, into the boiling sauce mixture. Cover and cook at full power for another 2 minutes, or until the shark is cooked through.

5. Remove from the oven, stir in the garam masala, replace the lid and leave to stand for 2 minutes before serving.

Serves 4

1 large onion, minced
2 large cloves garlic, crushed
1 tablespoon grated root ginger
1 green chilli, minced
1 teaspoon lemon juice
8 shark fillets, about 450 g/1 lb, skinned
2 tablespoons cooking oil
½ teaspoon turmeric powder
1 tablespoon ground coriander
1 teaspoon fennel (saunf) powder
2 teaspoons red chilli powder
1 tablespoon paprika
1 tablespoon tomato purée
salt, to taste
300 ml/½ pint/1¼ cups coconut milk
1 teaspoon garam masala

Prep 5 min
+ marinating time
Cooking 14 min
+ standing time 2 min

# Battakh Machhli aur Shimla Mirch

## BOMBAY DUCK WITH GREEN PEPPER

*Bombay duck is in fact a fish that looks like herring. They are found in abundance around the west coast of India. Unlike other fish, Bombay ducks like to swim on the surface of water, like ducks. They are cooked in many different ways. Here is a dry dish that is suitable for microwave cooking.*

**Serves 4**

1 tablespoon ghee
8 Bombay ducks, halved
1 large onion, finely chopped
1 green chilli, chopped
1 teaspoon ground coriander
1 teaspoon turmeric powder
1 teaspoon red chilli powder
2 cloves garlic, crushed
4 tomatoes, chopped
1 large green pepper, cut into
  strips
1 tablespoon desiccated
  coconut

**Prep 10 min**
**Cooking 13 min**
**+ standing time 5 min**

1. Place the ghee and Bombay ducks in a microwave-safe covered dish and cook on high for 2 minutes, turning over halfway through. Drain the fish and transfer it to a plate lined with kitchen paper.
2. To the remaining ghee, add the onion and cook, uncovered, at full power for 2 minutes. Stir in the green chilli, coriander, turmeric, chilli powder and garlic. Mix thoroughly and continue cooking, uncovered, on high for another 2 minutes.
3. Toss in the tomatoes, green pepper and the reserved Bombay ducks. Stir thoroughly. Cover and cook at full power for 7 minutes, or until the vegetables are cooked.
4. Remove from the oven, stir in the coconut and leave to stand, covered, for 5 minutes. Stir before serving with a curry, rice or chapatty and whatever else takes your fancy!

# Salaad, Kachumbar aur Raitay

SALADS, MISHMASHES AND RAITAS

An Indian meal looks wanting without a salad, mishmash or raita. The artistically presented raw, crisp and cool vegetables and fruits add a mélange of colour and lend character to your dining table. The main characteristic of these dishes is that they are so easy to make yet there is tremendous scope for experimentation. The use of many, easily available ingredients and seasonings produces a kaleidoscope of colours and flavours.

Most of these dishes are made outside the microwave but there are also those which have to be cooked in part. On offer in the following pages are a selection of dishes encompassing both types. Salads and mishmashes are similar in that both are made from standard and seasonal vegetables and fruits. Salads are usually a combination of a number of ingredients, moistened with oil, vinegar or a creamy sauce, before being seasoned and served on a bed of lettuce. Salads should be cool and crunchy even after dressing, so don't be too generous with dressing!

Mishmashes are made more quickly than salads. They are prepared basically by chopping or grating the main ingredients and serving them with the addition of seasonings and lemon juice.

Although salads and mishmashes can be made with one ingredient, such as cabbage or lettuce, it will add texture and flavour to the dish if several greens are used together. Some imagination is called for when selecting and combining the main ingredients. Garnishing is important too, especially if it improves the taste of the dish as well as enhancing its appearance.

Raitas are yoghurt-based dishes. They are made by mixing yoghurt with vegetables, fruits, herbs and spices and other seasonings. The main ingredient is processed first, then yoghurt is whisked, chosen seasonings are added and, as the grand finale, the raita is garnished, which does nothing if not make the dish more alluring!

Some Indian culinary etymologists believe, the word raita is derived from rai (mustard). They thus recommend a liberal use of mustard in the raita dishes, thereby lending a pungent, sour and oily texture to the dish. Others emphasize that ta (an abbreviation of taat, meaning 'hot') is the main kernel of the word. The followers of this school of thought therefore use a profusion of green chillies and red chilli powder in their raitas. Some others sauté their raitas with glazed mustard (see p.34) and additional red chillies or chilli powder.

A raita usually balances a meal by serving as an antidote to the accompanying hot and spicy dishes, is what I feel. The raitas also provide moisture that may be lacking in the foods with which they are served, such as kebabs or roasts. In order to further enhance the taste, raitas can be topped with sweet or sweet-and-sour sauces of your choice.

# Gobhi aur Gaajar Salaad

CAULIFLOWER AND CARROT SALAD

*This salad should please everyone because it offers scope for alternatives – for example, instead of potato, you may use satsuma. Serve in the company of pickles with a main meal or snack. The vinegar could be replaced with soured cream or lemon juice.*

1. Soak the lettuce in cold water for about 15 minutes, then dry and place in a plastic bag.
2. Clean and dice the cauliflower, carrots, boiled potatoes, white radish and green chillies. Place all these ingredients, as well as the lettuce and coriander leaves, in the refrigerator for at least 30 minutes, or until ready to serve.
3. Place two lettuce leaves on each individual serving plate. Neatly arrange the diced vegetables on the lettuce. Add a pinch of asafoetida, salt and cumin to each serving. Drizzle the vinegar over each salad, sprinkle with the coriander leaves and serve.

**Serves 4**

8 lettuce leaves
4 cauliflower florets
4 small carrots
4 medium potatoes, boiled
225 g/8 oz/ 1 cup white radish
2 small green chillies
2 tablespoons chopped coriander leaves
pinch of asafoetida powder
salt, to taste
1 teaspoon ground cumin
1 tablespoon cider vinegar

**Prep 15 min
+ boiling, soaking and chilling times**

# *Paneer aur Pyaaz Salaad*

## CHEESE AND ONION SALAD

**Serves 4**

8 crisp lettuce leaves
225 g/8 oz/1 cup fresh cream
  cheese (see p.38)
1 large onion
2 stalks of celery
1 green chilli
1 medium tomato
4 red radishes
4 tablespoons mayonnaise
salt, to taste
1 teaspoon mustard seeds,
  crushed

**Prep 20 min**
**+ soaking and chilling times**

*A distinctive salad that combines taste with looks, this also lends itself to experimentation. It should prove a popular dish with family and friends.*

1. Soak the lettuce in ice-cold water for 15 minutes, then remove from the water and refrigerate in a plastic bag.
2. Chop the cheese, onion, celery and green chilli. Cut the tomato into wedges and slice the radishes. Place the cheese and all the vegetables in the refrigerator for 30 minutes. Take them out when ready to serve.
3. Line a large glass serving bowl with lettuce. Dress the cheese, onion and celery with mayonnaise and place on top of the lettuce. Then sprinkle with the green chilli, salt and mustard. Garnish with the tomato and radish, and serve.

# Chukandar-Podina Salaad

MINTED BEETROOT SALAD

*This concoction is colourful and palatable. Serve it as a crisp side dish in the company of – or instead of – a yoghurt raita or chutney. Or serve it, in Western style, on its own.*

Serves 4

8 crisp lettuce leaves
2 medium beetroot
1 cucumber, about
   100 g/4 oz/1 cup
8 spring onions
2 tablespoons chopped mint
   leaves
mayonnaise, to dress
salt, to taste
1 teaspoon garam masala

Prep 15 min
+ soaking and chilling times

1. Soak the lettuce in cold water for 15 minutes. Drain, dry and put in a plastic bag.
2. Finely grate the beetroot, cucumber and onions. Place them in the refrigerator, together with the lettuce and mint leaves, for at least 30 minutes, or until ready to serve.
3. Remove the salad ingredients from the refrigerator and place two lettuce leaves on each individual serving dish. Arrange the beetroot, cucumber and onion over them. Dress with the mayonnaise and sprinkle each serving with some salt and garam masala. Top with the chopped mint and serve.

# Sabzi Salaad

THREE Cs SALAD

**Serves 4**

8 fresh lettuce leaves
2 stalks of celery
2 large carrots
2 red peppers
1 small onion
8 red radishes
2 large green chillies
salt, to taste
1 clove garlic, crushed
2 tablespoons cider vinegar
1 teaspoon sugar

**Prep 15 min**
**+ soaking and chilling times**

*This colourful salad soothes the eyes and pleases the palate. Instead of cabbage, capsicum (peppers) and cucumber, you may substitute other fruits and vegetables beginning with 'C', and you will still have a Three Cs salad. Also, you may process the vegetables differently – chop or grate them.*

1. Soak the lettuce in cold water for 15 minutes then drain and refrigerate in a plastic bag for 30 minutes or until ready to serve.
2. Chop the celery, carrots and peppers in such a way that you have long strips of them, rather like sticks. Peel and cut the onion into rings and slice the red radishes. Slice the chillies into long strips, too. Then refrigerate them all for half an hour, or until ready to serve.
3. Place two lettuce leaves on each individual serving dish. Then arrange the celery, carrots and peppers over the top and position the green chilli strips strategically on each plate. Sprinkle salt to taste over the preparation.
4. Combine garlic, vinegar and sugar in a small bowl, stirring to mix. Drizzle the liquid over each plate. Garnish each plate with onion rings and radish slices, adding more salt, if required. Serve with a meal.

# Adrak-Mirch Kachumbar

GINGER-CHILLI MISHMASH

*This is the easiest mishmash to make, but it is meant only for the chilli lovers – green chillies and ginger are both hot. It's not recommended for children or those with a delicate tongue! A great favourite of mine.*

1. Wash and dry the ginger and chillies. Peel the ginger and remove the stems from the chillies. Chop both into fine slices.
2. Place the ginger and chillies in a serving bowl, add the lemon juice and stir well. Sprinkle with the salt and pepper and blend thoroughly. Chill and serve with a meal.

Serves 4

50 g/2 oz root ginger
4 green chillies
2 tablespoons lemon juice
salt, to taste
pinch of freshly ground black
  pepper

Prep 10 min
+ chilling time

# Singhaara Kachumbar

## WATER-CHESTNUT AND FRIENDS

Serves 4

8 peeled water chestnuts
1 medium beetroot
2 carrots
4 cauliflower florets
4 tablespoons shredded
   cabbage
4 red radishes
salt, to taste
1 teaspoon red chilli powder
1 lemon

Prep 15 min
+ chilling time

*This is a very seasonal mishmash, even in India. Much depends on when and where the water chestnuts are available. For variety, or as an alternative, you may use boiled potatoes and cucumber. It's an attractive dish, either way.*

1. Finely grate the water chestnuts, beetroot, carrots and the cauliflower. Place in a serving bowl.
2. Add the cabbage and stir then slice the radishes and place them decoratively over the top. Sprinkle the mishmash with the salt and chilli powder, and squeeze the lemon all over. Chill before serving.

# Amrood aur Kela Kachumbar
## GUAVA AND BANANA MISHMASH

*An exotic mishmash par excellence! Although it is supposed to be served with a meal, children – and occasionally adults too – have been known to eat it on its own.*

1. Wash and dry the guavas and cucumber then chop them. Peel the banana and chop it up too. Place the chopped ingredients on a serving dish and add the asafoetida, salt and red chillies.
2. Drizzle the lemon juice over the preparation, stirring it. Garnish with coriander leaves, chill and serve.

**Serves 4**

4 small sweet guavas
1 cucumber, about 100g/
   4 oz/1 cup
1 ripe banana
pinch of asafoetida powder
salt, to taste
1 teaspoon crushed red
   chillies
4 tablespoons/⅓ cup
   lemon juice
2 tablespoons chopped
   coriander leaves

**Prep 15 min
+ chilling time**

# Tamaatar-Pyaaz Kachumbar

TOMATO AND ONION MISHMASH

Serves 4

4 firm, red tomatoes
8 spring onions
1 green chilli
1 tablespoon lemon juice
salt, to taste
pinch of red chilli powder
2 tablespoons chopped
    coriander leaves

Prep 15 min
+ chilling time (optional)

*Use spring onions in this dish for best results (ordinary onions come out second best). Make it fresh each time, for best flavour. Give it a quick chill and serve, or serve without chilling.*

1. Wash and dry the tomatoes, onions and green chilli. Chop them finely and place in a serving bowl.
2. Add the lemon juice and salt and blend thoroughly. Top with the chilli powder and coriander leaves. Chill, if desired, and serve.

# Paalak-Sarson Ka Raita

SPINACH AND MUSTARD RAITA

**This is a delicious and cooling side dish that balances a meal, if served with hot dishes.**

1. Pick over, wash and chop the spinach. In a microwave-proof dish, place the spinach and sufficient water to cover, and cook, uncovered, at full power for 4 minutes, or until the spinach wilts. Drain off the water and grind the spinach.
2. In a suitable shallow dish, place the ghee, mustard and green chilli and cook, covered, at full power for 3 minutes. Stir in the ground spinach and continue to cook, covered, for another 2 minutes. Leave to stand for 2 minutes.
3. In a serving bowl, whisk the yoghurt with some salt until smooth. Add the spinach mixture and blend thoroughly. Garnish with the chilli powder, chill and serve.

Serves 4

450 g/1 lb fresh spinach
1 teaspoon ghee
1 teaspoon mustard seeds, crushed
1 green chilli, finely chopped
300 ml/½ pint/1¼ cups, plain yoghurt
salt, to taste
1 teaspoon red chilli powder

Prep 15 min
+ chilling time
Cooking 9 min
+ standing time 2 min

# *Baigan aur Podina Raita*

MINTED AUBERGINE RAITA

**Serves 4**

1 large aubergine/eggplant
  about 450 g/1 lb
1 tablespoon ghee
salt, to taste
1 teaspoon red chilli powder
300 ml/½ pint/1¼ cups plain
  yoghurt
pinch of mustard powder
1 teaspoon white cumin
  seeds, roasted and ground
1 tablespoon shredded mint
  leaves

Prep 10 min
+ roasting and chilling times
Cooking 5 min
+ standing time 2 min

*This delectable raita may be a little unusual, though it is not generally unknown. Feel free to substitute any other comparable vegetables of your choice.*

1. Slice the aubergine into long strips. In a microwave-safe dish, heat the ghee, uncovered, at full power for 2 minutes. Add the aubergine, a pinch of salt and half the chilli powder and cook, covered, at full power for 3 minutes. Remove from the oven and set aside for 2 minutes.
2. In a deep bowl, whisk the yoghurt, some salt, the remaining chilli and the mustard powder to a smooth consistency. Add the aubergine and blend thoroughly. Garnish with the ground cumin and mint and serve chilled.

# Pyaaz Tamaatar Raita

TOMATO-SPRING ONION RAITA

**Spring onions and tomatoes provide a fine texture to this raita. If the consistency is too thick, add a little water.**

1. Chop the tomatoes and onions finely. In a bowl, whisk the yoghurt until it assumes a smooth consistency. Add the asafoetida, salt, green chilli and black pepper and beat again.
2. Stir the onion and tomato in the yoghurt mixture and blend thoroughly. Sprinkle with the cumin and mint and chill. Serve straight from the refrigerator.

Serves 4

2 firm tomatoes
4 spring onions
300 ml/½ pint/1¼ cups plain
  yoghurt
pinch of asafoetida powder
salt, to taste
1 fresh green chilli, chopped
pinch of freshly ground black
  pepper
1 teaspoon white cumin
  seeds, roasted and ground
1 tablespoon finely chopped
  mint leaves

Prep 15 min
+ roasting and chilling times

# Kakdi Raita

## CUCUMBER RAITA

Serves 4

1 green cucumber, about
175 g/6 oz
300 ml/½ pint/1¼ cups plain
yoghurt
1 green chilli
1 tablespoon coriander
leaves
salt, to taste
pinch of asafoetida powder
½ teaspoon mustard powder
1 teaspoon white cumin
seeds, roasted and ground

Prep 15 min
+ roasting and chilling times

*For the best taste, use the Indian variety of baby cucumbers (kakdi or kheera); the commonly available cucumber will do as second best. Serve this raita chilled, with a snack or full meal.*

1. Peel the cucumber and chop the flesh finely. Set aside. Grind the coriander leaves and green chilli together and set aside.
2. Whisk the yoghurt to a smooth consistency in a bowl. Add the salt, asafoetida, cucumber and coriander leaves and whisk again. Garnish tastefully with the mustard and cumin powders. Chill before serving.

# Kaddu aur Podina Raita

PUMPKIN AND FRESH MINT RAITA

*Pumpkin is a very common vegetable in India. It is easily available here in the West too and is not particularly expensive. However, the raita made from this common ingredient comes out deliciously uncommon indeed!*

1. Remove the outer skin and the stringy substance and seeds from inside the pumpkin: this will reduce its weight to just over 100g/4oz. Grate the pumpkin and carefully wash it.
2. Place the pumpkin in a microwave-compatible dish with water to cover. Cook, uncovered, at full power for 4 minutes. Remove from the oven and leave to stand for 2 minutes. When completely cool, gently squeeze the pumpkin flesh to remove all the water and set it aside.
3. Beat the yoghurt in a bowl until smooth. Stir in the salt, pepper and asafoetida and whisk again. Then add the pumpkin and blend with a spoon. Garnish with the garam masala and shredded mint. Chill and serve.

Serves 4

225 g/8 oz/2 cups green pumpkin
water, as required
300 ml/½ pint/1¼ cups plain yoghurt
salt, to taste
pinch of freshly ground black pepper
pinch of asafoetida powder
½ teaspoon garam masala
1 tablespoon shredded mint leaves

Prep 10 min
+ chilling time
Cooking 4 min
+ standing time 2 min

# *Boondi-Dhania Raita*

### BATTER-DROP AND CORIANDER RAITA

**Serves 4**

100 g/4 oz/1 cup batter drops
300 ml/½ pint/1¼ cups plain
  yoghurt
pinch of asafoetida powder
pinch of ground black pepper
salt, to taste
½ teaspoon garam masala
1 teaspoon red chilli powder
1 tablespoon finely chopped
  coriander leaves

**Prep 10 min**
**+ soaking and chilling times**

*This is a truly exotic yoghurt-based side dish. It tastes great anywhere, particularly if you top it with a sweet or sweet-and-sour sauce. Boondis (batter drops) are easily available from Asian grocers. If the raita is too thick, add a little water.*

1. Soak the batter drops in lukewarm water for 10-15 minutes, until they swell up and soften. Then gently squeeze out the water and set the batter drops aside.
2. Meanwhile, whisk the yoghurt and asafoetida together. When smooth, add the salt, black pepper and garam masala and beat thoroughly.
3. Add the batter drops and gently blend with a spoon. Garnish tastefully with the chilli powder and coriander leaves. Chill and serve straight from the refrigerator.

# Makhaana-Zeera Raita

LOTUS PUFFS-CUMIN RAITA

***If you are looking for an exotic antidote for the chilli hotness of your meal, this dish is it. And it is easy to digest as well.***

1. Clean and polish the lotus puffs, then crush them.
2. Use the ghee to grease the base of a microwave-friendly shallow dish and heat, covered, at full power for 2 minutes. Add the puffs together with a pinch of salt and cook, covered, on high for 2 minutes.
3. Meanwhile, beat the yoghurt to a smooth consistency in a deep bowl. Add more salt, if desired, and the chilli powder, if using. Stir in the lotus puffs and let them soak in.
4. Stir thoroughly then garnish with the cumin. Chill and serve straight from the refrigerator.

**Serves 4**

50 g/2 oz lotus puffs
1 teaspoon ghee
salt, to taste
300 ml/½ pint/1¼ cups plain
  yoghurt
small pinch of red chilli
  powder (optional)
1 tablespoon white cumin
  seeds, roasted and
  coarsely ground

**Prep 10 min**
**+ roasting and chilling times**
**Cooking 4 min**
**+ standing time 2 min**

# Santaron Ka Angoori Raita

SATSUMA AND GRAPE RAITA

Serves 4

16 satsuma segments
16 seedless grapes
300 ml/½ pint/1¼ cups plain
   yoghurt
1 teaspoon sugar, or to taste
1 teaspoon salt, or to taste
½ teaspoon green
   cardamom powder
1 teaspoon saffron strands,
   crushed
1 teaspoon red chilli powder

Prep 15 min
+ chilling time

*This sweet-and-sour delectation is of course a raita first, but it can also be served as dessert at the end of a main meal. You will be fascinated by its versatility in that you can substitute other fruits of your choosing. This dish has been my personal favourite from childhood, and one of the first dishes I ever put together.*

1. Peel the fibrous skin from the satsuma segments and remove the pips. Wash the grapes and halve them.
2. In a serving bowl, beat the yoghurt and sugar to a smooth consistency. Add the salt and cardamom powder and whisk again. Stir in the satsuma flesh and the grapes. Sprinkle the saffron and chilli powder on top. Chill and serve.

# Chatni, Raseeli aur Achaar

CHUTNEYS, SAUCES AND PICKLES

*Chutneys, sauces and pickles are an integral part of an Indian meal. Their common mission is to prod the sluggish appetites, titillate the taste buds and give a fillip to the flow of digestive juices.*

*They are made from fresh vegetables, fruits and, on occasion, with dried fruits and nuts, together with herbs and spices. In flavour, they can range from sweet to sour, through to sweet-and-sour. They can be hot or mild. Because of their pungency and contrasting flavours, they liven up any meal. They tend to tickle the palate, enhance the flavour of a meal and bring colour to your dining table – and your cheeks!*

*Chatni (written 'chutney' in English) means a preparation that can be 'licked' and is a term applied to various relishes and dips. Although chutneys are essentially Indian in origin, they can just as easily be served with Western foods, particularly those that have been grilled and roasted.*

*Chutneys are of two types: freshly ground (to last a day or two) and cooked (to last longer); some are also made by combining the two methods. The longer-lasting, cooked ones, tend to veer towards pickles, according to the Indian ethos. Western thinking, however, still tends to qualify them as chutneys. Most chutneys improve on chilling. They also become more acceptable when teamed imaginatively with snacks or meals, according to their aroma and flavour.*

*Sauces – cooked in full or in part – are thinner in consistency than chutneys. They are made in various ways from sugar, vinegar, water and milk. Whilst some sauces are served with specific dishes (such as saambhar or cumin sauces), most are served as toppings for various dishes.*

*To prevent sauces from boiling over in the microwave, always use a large dish or jug about 3 times the measure of the contents, and grease the sides of the cooking dish with ghee or oil right up to the brim. When the sauce is ready, it should be stored in a clean, dry, sterilized and airtight container. It should be covered tightly after each use so that the contents remain fresh and last longer. Keep the container in a cool place.*

*Pickles with an Indian meal are like make-up on the face of a pretty girl: it makes her even more ravishing; similarly, pickles make you even more ravenous! But just as over-use of make-up spoils the impact, pickles must also be served in moderation.*

*Pickles have been made in India for hundreds of centuries – usually made in large quantities once a year. There are also pickles which are instant and can be made quickly (lasting a few days). Some mature over a few days and last a few weeks. But those which take a couple of weeks or more to mature last almost for ever! Unfortunately, the last category requires excruciating care and caution. Given that few people have got that sort of time these days, I have omitted them.*

*The preserving agents used in Indian pickles are salt, lemon juice, vinegar, spices and oil –individually or in combination. Most of the long-lasting pickles are made from oil; any vegetable oil is fine, but mustard oil is preferred, because of the colour and flavour it brings to the pickle. Sweet pickles have sugar and molasses added to them. Many Indian pickles, like wines, mature with time and thus attain a pinnacle of perfection in flavour.*

# Rewatcheeni aur Gud Ki Chatni

RHUBARB AND JAGGERY CHUTNEY

*Most of the ingredients in this recipe are freely used in Western kitchens, and yet it produces a typically Eastern flavour! Serve as a side dish with an Indian or Western meal. This chutney, put in the refrigerator in a covered container, lasts 7 to 10 days.*

1. Place the rhubarb, water and jaggery in a microwave-proof dish and cook, uncovered, at full power for 4 minutes.
2. Add the asafoetida, garam masala, nigella, garlic and ginger, stir and cook, half-covered, at full power for 3 minutes.
3. Stir and add the salt and chilli powder. Continue cooking, half-covered, on high for another 3 minutes.
4. Stir in the lemon juice, cover, and cook on high for 5 more minutes.
5. Remove from the oven and leave to stand for 5 minutes. When cool, serve with snacks or meals as desired. Leftovers can go into the refrigerator, in a covered container.

Serves 10

225 g/8 oz/2 cups rhubarb, ready weight
600 ml/1 pint/2½ cups water
100 g/4 oz/1 cup jaggery
pinch of asafoetida powder
1 teaspoon garam masala
½ teaspoon nigella (kalaunji)
1 clove garlic, sliced
½ teaspoon grated root ginger
salt, to taste
½ teaspoon red chilli powder
1 tablespoon lemon juice

Prep 10 min
Cooking 15 min
+ standing time 5 min

# Naariyal Chatni
## Coconut Chutney

**Serves 4**

2 tablespoons grated fresh
  coconut
large pinch of cumin powder
  (page 26)
2 tablespoons mixed daals:
  urad and chana (black
  beans & grams), dry
  roasted and ground
1 teaspoon shredded root
  ginger
2 green chillies, ground
12 curry leaves, finely
  chopped (or coriander
  or mint leaves)
2 teaspoons salt, or to taste
1 tablespoon lemon juice
1 tablespoon melted ghee
  (or vegetable oil)
2 teaspoons yellow mustard
  seeds, whole

**Prep 10 min + chilling time**
**Cooking 3 min**
**+ standing time 2 min**

*This chutney is frequently seved with south Indian dishes, often in tandem with saambhar (p.180). Some people prefer to use plain yoghurt (3 tablespoons), instead of lemon juice. When kept in a covered container in the refrigerator, this chutney lasts for upto a fortnight, and several months in the freezer.*

1. In a bowl, place all the ingredients from coconut to curry leaves and mix thoroughly. Then add the salt and lemon juice and blend.
2. In a micsrowave-safe covered skillet or dish, place the ghee (or oil) and heat at full power for 3 minutes. Remove from the oven, add the mustard and replace the lid for 10-15 seconds. Remove the lid and stir rapidly, then add the whole lemon-infused mixture to the dish and blend. Replace the lid and leave to stand for 2 minutes.
3. Transfer the contents into a serving bowl. Chill before serving.

# Kachche Lukaat Ki Chatni
GREEN LOQUAT CHUTNEY

*A real scoop for the lovers of the exotic! Persuade your Asian greengrocer to obtain some loquats, and a fantastic taste comes to your dining table with this sour chutney. Serve with a bland meal or savoury snack.*

1. Wash and dry the loquats, then halve them and remove the seeds. Grind coarsely together with the mint, chillies, cumin and salt on a sil-batta, or use a pestle and mortar or an electric grinder.
2. Place the mixture in a serving bowl. Add enough water to obtain a thick consistency. Refrigerate for at least 30 minutes before serving.

**Serves 4**

8 green loquats
50 g/2 oz mint leaves
2 small green chillies, chopped
1 teaspoon white cumin seeds
salt, to taste
water, as required

Prep 5 min
+ chilling time

# Kamrakh Ki Chatni

BABACO AND MINT CHUTNEY

**Serves 4**

4 ripe babacoes
20 mint leaves
1 fresh green chilli, chopped
pinch of white cumin seeds
pinch of mustard seeds
salt, to taste
water, as necessary

**Prep 5 min**
**+ chilling time**

*An exotic chutney par excellence! A babaco (also called star fruit and carambola), when ripe, is a large, yellow, rocket-shaped fruit with soft, juicy ribs. It tastes exotically of strawberries and pineapple rolled into one. It is now relatively easily available, even in supermarkets. If the chutney is too thick for you, add a little water or lemon juice.*

1. Top and tail the babacoes, remove the seeds and chop the flesh. Place the fruit, mint leaves, green chillies, cumin seeds, mustard seeds and salt in a mortar and pound to a pulp with the pestle. Alternatively, use a sil-batta.
2. Stir water into the mixture until you have the desired consistency. Refrigerate for 30 minutes before serving. Leftovers can go back to the refrigerator.

# Karonda aur Dhania Ki Chatni

GOOSEBERRY-CORIANDER CHUTNEY

*For best results, obtain from your grocer the genuine Indian karondas – roughly equated with gooseberries or cranberries. The consistency of this exotic sour chutney is controlled by the addition of water. It is very suitable for picnics and parties. Otherwise, serve as a side dish with a main meal. The chutney lasts a couple of days.*

1. Wash and dry the gooseberries; halve them and remove the seeds. Place the fruit together with the coriander leaves, cumin and green chilli, into a mortar and crush with the pestle into a coarse mixture (or use the traditional sil-batta, or an electric grinder).
2. Add the salt and chilli powder and pound a little more. Pour in the requisite amount of water and blend, bringing the chutney to the desired consistency. Chill for about 30 minutes before serving.

**Serves 8**

225 g/8 oz/1 cup
   gooseberries
2 tablespoons chopped
   coriander leaves
pinch of white cumin seeds
1 green chilli, chopped
salt, to taste
½ teaspoon red chilli
   powder
water, as required

**Prep 10 min
+ chilling time**

# Amrood aur Neebu Ki Chatni

GUAVA AND LEMON CHUTNEY

**Serves 8**

4 ripe, medium-sized guavas
2 tablespoons mint leaves
2 small green chillies
½ teaspoon sliced root
   ginger
salt, to taste
6 tablespoons/½ cup lemon
   juice

**Prep 10 min
+ chilling time**

*This is an excellent sweet and sour chutney. Buy fresh, ripe guavas, which are available almost everywhere now, and the chutney you make will taste out of this world! Adjust the consistency to your liking by using more or less lemon juice. Serve as a side dish with a main meal, or with a snack.*

1. Wash and dry the guavas, mint and chillies, then chop. Place them, together with the ginger and salt, on a sil and grind coarsely with the batta (or use another grinder).
2. Transfer the thick pulp to a serving bowl. Add the lemon juice and blend thoroughly. Chill for 30 minutes and serve.

# Anannaas aur Chhuhaara Ki Chatni
## PINEAPPLE ON A DATE

*It may come as a surprise to Western readers, but a truly delicious and mysteriously exotic sweet and sour relish can be prepared by combining pineapple with dates and plums. You can serve it as a dip with western food also.*

1. Soak the dates, plums and sultanas in warm water for 4 hours. Then drain off the water and removes the pits, stones and seeds. Chop the flesh of the reconstituted fruit.
2. Place the pineapple, dates, plums and sultanas in a microwave-safe lidded casserole. Add sufficient water to cover and cook, uncovered, at full power for 6 minutes, or until the water comes to a boil.
3. Stir in the turmeric and mustard and blend well. Add the sugar, salt and lemon juice. Cover and cook, at full power, for another 6 minutes, stirring once or twice. The mixture should be well blended.
4. Take the casserole out of the oven, remove the lid, sprinkle the mixture with the cardamom and chilli powder. Replace the lid, and leave to stand for 5 minutes. Serve when cool. Leftovers can go into the refrigerator for subsequent use.

Serves 8

2 dried dates
4 dried plums
1 tablespoon sultanas/raisins
225 g/8 oz/2 cups pineapple
  flesh, chopped
water, as required
½ teaspoon turmeric powder
1 teaspoon mustard powder
1 tablespoon raw cane sugar
salt, to taste
2 tablespoons lemon juice
pinch of green cardamom
  powder
pinch of red chilli powder

Prep 10 min
+ soaking and chilling times
Cooking 12 min
+ standing time 5 min

# Seib-Anannaas Paani

APPLE-PINEAPPLE SAUCE

**Serves 10**

2 sweet apples
225 g/8 oz/2 cups pineapple
   flesh, chopped
600 ml/1 pint/2½ cups water
2 tablespoons sugar
½ teaspoon salt
4 cloves, ground
pinch of green cardamom
   powder
pinch of saffron strands,
   crushed

**Prep 15 min**
**Cooking 13 min**
**+ standing time 5 min**

*This is a delightful sweet sauce which, with a thicker consistency, can be served with savoury snacks or as a side dish with a main meal. Make it thinner and it could become a very likeable drink by itself! It is usually served cold.*

1. Peel, core and chop the apples and place them and the pineapple in a microwave-safe casserole of 1.8 litre/3 pint/7½ cup capacity. Pour in the measured water and cook, uncovered, at full power for 8 minutes, or until the apple is tender.
2. Take the casserole away from the heat. Mash the contents together and push through a fine sieve. Transfer the mixture back to the casserole and return to the microwave.
3. Stir in the remaining ingredients (saffron last) and cook, half-covered, at full power for 5 minutes, or until the desired consistency is obtained.
4. Remove from the oven and leave to stand, fully covered, for 5 minutes. Serve hot or cold. When completely cool, pack in a dry, sterilized jar or bottle for later use. Cover the container after each use and store in a cool place such as the refrigerator.

# Aadu-Khubaani Sirka

## PEACH-APRICOT VINEGAR SAUCE

*This is a rather classy sauce, with a consistency that can be adapted to personal preference. Serve as a side dish with a main meal. It should prove popular with connoisseurs and novices alike.*

1. Wash and dry the peaches and apricots, then pit them and chop the flesh. Clean, dry and chop the sultanas, too.
2. In a microwave-safe lidded casserole of 2.4 litre/4 pint/10 cup capacity, place the peaches, apricots, sultanas and tomatoes. Cook, half-covered, at full power for 5 minutes or until the ingredients are well blended.
3. Remove from the oven, mash the contents and stir to obtain a smooth consistency. Push the liquid through a fine sieve or a piece of muslin.
4. Transfer the mixture back to the casserole and return to the microwave. Add the vinegar and the remaining ingredients – one by one – and cook, half-covered, at full power for 8 minutes, or until the sauce is of the required consistency.
5. Leave the sauce to stand, fully covered, for 5 minutes. Serve hot or cold. Store in a sterilized container for later use.

**Makes 600 ml/1 pint/2½ cups**

2 peaches, about 225 g/8 oz/ 2 cups
4 apricots, about 225g /8oz/ 2 cups
1 tablespoon sultanas/raisins
4 ripe tomatoes, chopped
600 ml/1 pint/2½ cups cider vinegar
225 g/8 oz/1 cup sugar
salt, to taste
½ teaspoon red chilli powder
6 cloves garlic, chopped
50 g/2 oz grated root ginger
pinch of ground nutmeg
pinch of ground cinnamon
pinch of ground cloves

**Prep 10 min**
**Cooking 13 min**
**+ standing time 5 min**

# Zeera Paani

## CUMIN SAUCE

Makes 600 ml/1 pint/2½ cups

100 g/4 oz/2 cups seedless
  tamarind pulp
600 ml/1 pint/2½ cups
  lukewarm water
1 green chilli
25 g/1 oz mint leaves
½ teaspoon grated root
  ginger
salt, to taste
pinch of black salt
½ teaspoon red chilli
  powder
½ teaspoon cumin powder
1 teaspoon garam masala
1 tablespoon lemon juice

Prep 15 min
+ soaking and chilling times

*This sauce is usually served with the chaat dish called golgappa or puchka, but it can also be served by itself, as an appetizer and refreshing drink, particularly in the hot weather – in that case, add crushed ice to each serving. This is a popular sauce and has been made in many parts of India since ancient times. It is made from many recipes; this is one of the better ones. I hope you like it.*

1. Soak the tamarind in the warm water for 30 minutes, then mash it thoroughly. Push the liquid through a fine sieve or a muslin cloth into a bowl, and discard the remaining husk. (You could buy bottled tamarind juice, but you can't always be sure of quality.)
2. Grind the green chilli, mint and ginger together with the salt. Add the paste to the strained tamarind juice and stir thoroughly until blended.
3. Add the red chilli powder, ground cumin and garam masala and whisk briskly for a few seconds. Mix in the lemon juice and refrigerate for at least 30 minutes before serving.

# Tamaatar Sirka

TOMATO VINEGARY SAUCE

*This is an exotic Oriental sauce which is nothing like its bottled cousins sold in Western supermarkets. It is handy to have around the house; serve it with savoury snacks*

1. Mash the tomatoes in a microwave-safe casserole of 1.8 litre/3 pint/7½ cup capacity. Add the sugar and cook, uncovered, at full power for 3 minutes, stirring once.
2. Chop the garlic, ginger and sultanas and add them to the casserole. Stir thoroughly. Pour in the vinegar and all the remaining ingredients. Cook, half-covered, at full power for 7 minutes.
3. Remove the casserole from the oven and let it stand, covered, for 5 minutes. When cool, store the sauce in an air-tight container and keep in a cool place. Cover the container tightly after each use.

**Makes 600 ml/1 pint/2½ cups**

900 g/2 lb ripe tomatoes, peeled
450 g/1 lb/2 cups sugar
100 g/4 oz garlic cloves
100 g/4 oz root ginger, peeled and chopped
2 teaspoons sultanas/raisins
300 ml/½ pint/1¼ cups cider vinegar
salt, to taste
1 teaspoon red chilli powder
pinch of garam masala

**Prep 15 min**
**Cooking 10 min**
**+ standing time 5 min**

# Saambhar

## VEGELENTIL SAUCE

Makes 600 ml/1 pint/2½ cups

2 tablespoons brown grams
water, as required
225 g/8 oz/1 cup mixed
   lentils, such as toor and
   urad
salt, as required
pinch of turmeric powder
1 tablespoon mustard oil
pinch of asafoetida powder
1 green chilli, chopped
1 tablespoon grated onion
1 tablespoon saambhar
   powder (see p. 28)
225 g/8 oz/2 cups mixed
   vegetables, diced
1 tablespoon desiccated
   coconut
1 tablespoon lemon juice
1 tablespoon chopped
   coriander leaves

Prep 15 min
+ soaking time
Cooking 22 min
+ standing time 5 min

*This sauce is the inevitable companion of many south Indian dishes and plain rice preparations. Use seasonal vegetables of your choice for this dish and adjust the amount of water to your own liking.*

1. Soak the grams and lentils, separately, in water for at least 4 hours. Drain off the water. Set the lentils aside and coarsely grind the grams.

2. Place the lentils together with 1 teaspoon of salt and a pinch of turmeric in a microwave-safe casserole of 1.8 litre/3 pint/7½ cup capacity. Pour in 600ml/1 pint/2½ cups of water and cook, uncovered, at full power for 10 minutes, or until the water comes to a rolling boil. Stir occasionally during cooking.

3. In a shallow microwavable dish, place the mustard oil, asafoetida, chilli and onion and cook, uncovered, on high for 3 minutes. Stir in the saambhar powder and the ground grams and continue to cook, half-covered, at full power for another 3 minutes, stirring once.

4. Add this mixture to the casserole. Pour in additional water to taste – possibly around 300ml/½ pint/1¼ cups – and add more salt, if required. Stir thoroughly.

5. Add the vegetables, cover and cook at full power for another 6 minutes, or until the vegetables are tender and the mixture is well blended.

6. Remove the casserole from the oven. Lift the lid and stir in the coconut and lemon juice. Quickly replace the lid and leave to stand for 5 minutes. Garnish with the coriander leaves and serve as desired.

# Sonth

GINGERY MANGO SAUCE

*This sweet and sour sauce is often served as a side dish but it can also be served as a topping for yoghurt-based savouries and chaat dishes. A good means of producing colour contrasts on the dining table.*

1. Place the sultanas, dates and ginger in a bowl, cover with tap water and soak for about 1 hour. Drain and set aside.
2. Place the dried green mango slices, measured water and molasses in a microwave-compatible casserole of 1.8 litre/3 pint/7½ cup capacity. Cook, half-covered, at full power for 8 minutes, or until the mango slices are tender. Stir once or twice during cooking.
3. Take the casserole out of the oven. Mash the contents together and push them through a fine sieve. Transfer the mixture back to the casserole and add the sultanas, dates, ginger and all the remaining ingredients. Stir thoroughly, cover and cook at full power for another 10 minutes, stirring a couple of times during the cooking period.
4. Remove the casserole from the oven and let it stand, covered, for 5 minutes. Serve the sauce hot or cold. When cool, store in a sterilized jar or bottle.

Serves 10

2 tablespoons sultanas/raisins
2 tablespoons chopped
  dry dates
1 tablespoon sliced root
  ginger
100 g/4 oz/1 cup dried green
  mango slices
600 ml/1 pint/2½ cups water
225 g/8 oz/1 cup molasses
  (gur)
salt, to taste
½ teaspoon coarsely ground
  coriander seeds
pinch of garam masala
1 teaspoon red chilli powder

Prep 15 min
+ soaking time
Cooking 18 min
+ standing time 5 min

# Aam Ka Panna

MANGO AND MINT SAUCE

Serves 4

4 green mangoes
water, as required
1 tablespoon sugar
1 teaspoon salt, or to taste
½ teaspoon red chilli
  powder
50 g/2 oz fresh mint leaves,
  ground
½ teaspoon ground cumin

Prep 15 min
+ chilling time
Cooking 8 min
+ standing time 5 min

*This is a magical dish which serves as a drink in itself, and also as sauce to add variety to the taste of a dish. Adjust the amount of water and the condiments to your liking. As a drink, it cools you down in the summer and tastes sweet and sour. As a sauce, it tastes out of this world!*

1. Place the mangoes and sufficient water to fully cover them in a microwave-proof covered dish of 1.2 litre/2 pint/5 cup capacity. Cook, covered, on high for 8 minutes, or until the water has come to a boil. Remove from the heat and leave to cool for 5 minutes. Then drain off the water and peel, stone and pulp the mangoes in a deep bowl (you could use ready-made raw mango pulp – no guarantees of quality, though!).

2. To the pulp, add sugar and 150-300 ml/½ pint/1¼ cups of water to make a sauce. (To make a drink, add 600 ml/1 pint /2½ cups of water.) Whisk thoroughly.

3. Stir in the salt, red chilli powder and ground mint and whisk again. Add the ground cumin and blend well. Chill in the refrigerator for 30 minutes before serving. To serve as a drink, pour the mixture into tall glasses and serve topped with crushed ice.

# Aam Ka Chhoonda

SWEET MANGO SHREDS

*This is one of the easiest and quickest recipes for a sweet mango pickle. It takes about a week to mature in the sun; slightly longer otherwise. Children love it, and start sampling it even before it is ready.*

1. Peel the mangoes and shred the flesh. Stir in the salt and asafoetida and blend thoroughly.
2. On a microwavable plate, place the cumin, fennel and coriander seeds, spreading them out evenly. Roast, uncovered, in the microwave at full power for 2 minutes then grind coarsely. Add the chilli powder and sugar and mix well.
3. Place the mangoes in a clean, dry jar or crock. Add the spice-sugar mixture, cover with the lid or a muslin cloth and shake well.
4. Put the jar out in the sun for about 1 week. When the sugar has blended with the rest of the ingredients to give a golden, thick syrup, the pickle is ready. (In the absence of sun, mature the pickle in the warmest place in the house – it will then take a little longer to mature.)
5. Shake the jar at least once a day. Cover tightly after each use so as not to let in any air.

Serves 10

225 g/8 oz/2 cups green
   mangoes
salt, to taste
pinch of asafoetida powder
1 teaspoon white cumin
   seeds
1 teaspoon fennel seeds
1 teaspoon coriander seeds
1 teaspoon red chilli powder
225 g/8 oz/1 cup raw cane
   sugar

**Prep 15 min**
**+ maturing time**
**Cooking 2 min**

# Shaljum aur Seim Ka Meetha Achaar
## SWEET TURNIPS AND GREEN BEANS

**Serves 20**

225 g/8 oz/2 cups turnips
225 g/8 oz/2 cups green beans
  (seim)
150 ml/¼ pint/⅔ cup
  mustard oil
salt, to taste
½ teaspoon red chilli
  powder
1 teaspoon mustard powder
1 teaspoon ground cinnamon
1 teaspoon ground cumin
4 tablespoons malt vinegar
100 g/4 oz/1 cup molasses
  (gur)
150 ml/¼ pint/⅔ cup
  lukewarm water

**Prep 15 min
+ maturing time
Cooking 10 min
+ standing time 2 min**

*This preparation combines the cooking and sunning processes to produce a stunning pickle. It lasts for several weeks. A delightful side dish, capable of bringing a lifeless, dull meal to life!*

1. Peel the turnips and cut them and the beans into small pieces. Place in a microwave-proof casserole with sufficient water to cover. Cook, uncovered, in the microwave at full power for 4 minutes. Remove from the oven and drain off the water.
2. Place the parboiled vegetables in a deep bowl. Add the mustard oil, salt, chilli powder, mustard powder, cinnamon and cumin and blend thoroughly.
3. Put the spiced vegetable mixture in a dry sterilized jar or crock. Add the vinegar, cover the mouth of the jar with a lid or muslin cloth, and put it out in the sun for 1 week until the mixture turns sour (or keep in the warmest place in the house, where it will take a while longer).
4. Place the molasses and the measured water in a microwave-safe casserole and cook, half-covered, at full power for 6 minutes, or until the water comes to a boil. Remove from the oven and let it stand for 2 minutes.
5. Add the sweet liquid to the pickle jar, stir and put it out in to the sun for another week. Serve when required, covering the jar after each use.

# Gobhi Hari Matar Achaar

PICKLED CAULIFLOWER AND GREEN PEAS

*Fresh vegetables are ideal for this pickle but frozen ones will do too, as an alternative. You may substitute other vegetables of your choice, for example turnip, potato, carrot. One can use vinegar or lemon juice instead of oil. Anyone can make this pickle; everyone likes it!*

1. Cut the cauliflower into small pieces and shell the peas: choose the proportion of the two vegetables according to your personal preference. Place the vegetables in a microwave-friendly casserole and add sufficient water to cover. Cook, without covering, at full power for 4 minutes then drain off the water, sprinkle with 1 teaspoon of salt and leave to dry.

2. Place the coriander, fennel and fenugreek seeds on a microwave-proof plate, spreading them out evenly. Roast, uncovered, at full power for 2 minutes then coarsely grind using a sil-batta or other grinder. Mix with the turmeric, asafoetida and mango powders.

3. Take a clean, dry and sterilized jar or crock and place the vegetables in it. Add the spice mixture and additional salt to taste. Shake thoroughly. Pour in the mustard oil and shake the container again to blend the ingredients.

4. Cover with a lid or a clean muslin cloth and put the pickle out in the sun (or the warmest place in the house) for 2 to 3 days. Alternatively, heat the oil for 2 minutes at full power before use. Shake the jar or crock at least once a day; cover it after each use.

Serves 20

450 g/1 lb ready weight mixture of cauliflower and green peas
water, as required
salt, to taste
1 tablespoon coriander seeds
1 tablespoon fennel seeds
1 teaspoon fenugreek seeds
1 teaspoon turmeric powder
pinch of asafoetida powder
1 tablespoon mango powder (aamchoor)
150 ml/¼ pint/⅔ cup mustard oil

Prep 20 min
+ drying and maturing times
Cooking 6 min

# Aam Ka Noncha

CORNED MANGOES

Serves 20

450 g/1 lb green mangoes
1 teaspoon asafoetida
  powder
1 teaspoon red chilli powder
large pinch of ground cumin
1 tablespoon salt

Prep 10 min
+ maturing time

*This pickle must be the easiest to make, and has a haunting taste. It is sure to inject life into the blandest of meals. The preparation is suitable for picnics and parties. Adjust the quantity of salt, chilli and asafoetida, the main flavouring ingredients of this pickle, to your liking.*

1. Peel the mangoes and cut the flesh of each into 4 or 8 pieces, depending on the size of the fruit. Place the mangoes in a large bowl or on a platter. Add the rest of the ingredients, one by one, blending thoroughly.
2. Take a dry and sterilized covered glass jar and place the spiced mango pieces in it. Sprinkle on some more salt, if desired, and cover tightly with the lid. Place the jar out in the sun for about a week. Don't forget to bring the jar indoors at night.
3. When the pickle matures – becomes a little sticky – and all the ingredients are well blended, serve as required. Shake the jar once a day. Close the lid after each use.

# Bhuni Mirch Ka Achaar

SAUTÉED CHILLI PICKLE

*This is truly an instant pickle. Serve it hot or cold, soon after it is made. It is convenient to make this pickle while preparing stuffed vegetables such as aubergine or okra. If you have the spices ready, you may make this pickle whenever you buy green chillies.*

1. Wipe the chillies with a damp cloth. Keeping their stalks, slit them lengthways. Scoop out the insides and set them aside separately from the pods.
2. Place the nigella, fenugreek, coriander seeds, mango powder, fennel seeds and salt on a suitable dinner plate and spread them out evenly. Roast in the microwave, at full power and without cover, for 2 minutes then grind them. Add the insides of the chillies and half the mustard oil and mix thoroughly.
3. Fill the chilli pods with this stuffing. Any leftover spice mixture should be spread over the chillies when they are cooking.
4. With the remaining teaspoon of mustard oil, grease the base of a microwave-compatible shallow dish. Position the stuffed chillies on the dish, cover and cook at full power for 2 minutes, or until the chillies are cooked. Turn over once during the cooking time.
5. Remove from the oven and serve hot or cold with a snack or meal.

Serves 10

100 g/4 oz/1 cup green chillies
pinch of nigella (kalaunji)
pinch of fenugreek seeds (methi)
1 teaspoon coriander seeds
1 teaspoon mango powder (aamchoor)
1 teaspoon fennel seeds
pinch of salt, or to taste
2 teaspoons mustard oil

Prep 10 min
Cooking 4 min

# Khat-Mitthee Mirch

## SWEET AND SOUR CHILLI

Serves 10

225 g/8 oz/1 cup green
  chillies
2 teaspoons ghee
pinch of turmeric powder
pinch of asafoetida powder
100 g/4 oz/1 cup molasses
  (gur)
150 ml/¼ pint/⅔ cup water
1 teaspoon grated root ginger
2 cloves garlic, sliced
½ teaspoon fennel
salt, to taste
3 tablespoons/¼ cup lemon
  juice
½ teaspoon garam masala

Prep 10 min
Cooking 14 min
+ standing time 5 min

*This pickle, made from green chillies, is strangely sweet and sour! It is instant and requires no maturing time so you may serve it as soon as it is cooked. A tasty pickle which lasts for several days.*

1. Slice the chillies into thin strips.
2. In a microwave-friendly casserole of 1.2 litre/2 pint/5 cup capacity, place the ghee, turmeric and asafoetida and cook, uncovered, at full power for 2 minutes.
3. Add the molasses and the measured water and cook, half-covered, on high for 6 minutes, or until the water boils.
4. Drop in the chillies, together with all the rest of the ingredients – one by one. Continue to cook, covered, at full power for another 6 minutes, or until the water evaporates and the pickle assumes the desired thick consistency.
5. Remove from the oven and leave to stand, covered, for 5 minutes. Then serve as needed. Store any leftovers in a covered jar for subsequent use. Cover the container after each use.

# Neebu Ka Meetha Achaar

SWEET LEMON PICKLE

*Use thin-skinned (kaaghazi) lemons of medium size for this pickle. Because of the combination of cooking and sunning, this pickle matures quickly. It can last for several weeks, or even months, provided of course that you make enough to go that far!*

1. Wash, dry and quarter the lemons but do not peel them. Remove the pips.
2. In a microwave-compatible casserole of 1.2 litre/2 pint/5 cup capacity, place the oil, sugar, salt and turmeric and cook, half-covered, at full power for 3 minutes, stirring once.
3. Add the lemons, together with all the remaining ingredients – one by one. Continue to cook, covered, at full power for 6 minutes, or until the oil separates. Remove from the oven and leave to stand, covered, for 5 minutes.
4. Transfer the mixture to a suitable dry, sterilized-lidded jar or crock. Place the jar, uncovered, in the sun for 2 to 3 days and the pickle will be ready. Then cover the jar and keep it in a warm place. Serve the lemons as required, covering the jar after each use. Shake the container at least once a day.

Serves 20

5 juicy lemons
150 ml/¼ pint/⅔ cup vegetable oil
50 g/2 oz/¼ cup raw cane sugar
salt, to taste
½ teaspoon turmeric powder
½ teaspoon red chilli powder
4 cloves
1 teaspoon fennel seeds
½ teaspoon garam masala

Prep 10 min
+ maturing time
Cooking 9 min
+ standing time 5 min

# Murabbay

PRESERVES

Preserves are a popular form of confection in India. Unlike ordinary sweetmeats, they last a long time – sometimes up to a year and beyond – and come in handy when that unexpected guest arrives!

Wholesome and sustaining, preserves are generally made from fruits or vegetables. They boast delicious flavours and are normally served decorated with edible silver or gold foils to match the colour of the dish. They should be stored, at room temperature, in dry, sterilized, airtight jars until required.

The preparation of these preserves involves cleaning the fruit or vegetable, pricking them with a fork or cocktail stick – to increase the soaking capacity – boiling them in water and then immersing in sugar syrup. The syrup required for these preserves is usually of 2-string consistency (see page 39). However, you may use a syrup, ready prepared, of 1-string strength and get to the required consistency by further boiling.

Preserves are best served first thing in the morning. They are said to have soothing properties and are good for the heart and for refreshing the brain.

# Santaray Ka Murabba

SATSUMA PRESERVE

Serves 4-8

4 juicy satsumas
2 teaspoons slaked lime
water, as necessary
300 ml/½ pint/1¼ cups
   sugar syrup of 1-string
   strength (see p.39)
kewra water, to sprinkle
gold foils, to decorate

Prep 10 min
Cooking 15 min
+ standing time 5 min
Storage 30 days (minimum)

*This tongue-tingling confection is sheer heaven first thing in the morning. It refreshes and prepares you to face the world! You can also make a similar dish with an alternative main ingredient: lemons (use 8).*

1. Peel the satsumas and gently prick them all over with a cocktail stick to make them porous. Place in a microwave-safe 1.2 litre/2 pint/5 cup lidded dish, together with the slaked lime and sufficient water to submerge the fruit. Cook, uncovered, on high for 5 minutes.
2. Remove the dish from the oven and drain off the water. Gently rinse the satsumas in several changes of cold water and dry them completely.
3. In the same cooking dish, place the sugar syrup and cook, uncovered, at full power for 5 minutes, stirring once. Skim any scum from the surface.
4. Carefully add the satsumas to the syrup. Cover with kitchen paper and continue to cook, at full power, for a further 5 minutes, or until the syrup thickens and the satsumas are cooked. Stir carefully once or twice during the cooking phase.
5. Remove the dish from the oven and leave it to stand for 5 minutes. Store the mixture in a sterilized, airtight jar. Serve hot or cold, sprinkling each serving with kewra water and garnishing with a gold foil.

# Naashpaati Ka Murabba

PEAR PRESERVE

*If you want to push your brain into top gear early in the morning, you can't go wrong with a few mouthfuls of this tasty preserve before breakfast. Feel free to use plantain instead of pears.*

1. Peel the pears and cut off their tops and bottoms. Prick them all over with a fork and place in a microwave-friendly 1.2 litre/2 pint/5 cup lidded dish with enough water to cover. Cook, uncovered, at full power for 5 minutes. Remove from the heat and drain off the water. Transfer the pears to a plate.

2. Pour the sugar syrup into the same cooking dish and heat, uncovered, at full power for 5 minutes, stirring halfway through. Skim as necessary then carefully add the pears, cover, and continue to cook on high for another 5 minutes, or until the syrup thickens and the pears are cooked. Stir carefully once or twice during this cooking period.

3. Remove the dish from the oven and leave to stand for 5 minutes. Meanwhile, steep the saffron in the rose water and sprinkle over the pears. Store in a sterilized, airtight jar. Serve hot or cold, decorated with gold foils.

Serves 4-8

4 medium-sized firm pears
water, as necessary
300 ml/½ pint/1¼ cups
    sugar syrup of 1-string
    strength (see p.39)
pinch of saffron, crushed
1 tablespoon rose water
gold foils, to decorate

Prep 10 min
Cooking 15 min
+ standing time 5 min
Storage 6 months (minimum)

# Mooli Ka Murabba

## WHITE RADISH PRESERVE

Serves 4-8

225 g/8 oz/2 cups
white radish,
ready weight
water, as necessary
600 ml/1 pint/2½ cups sugar
syrup of 1-string strength
(see p.39)
1 tablespoon rose water
silver foils, to decorate

Prep 10 min
Cooking 15 min
+ standing time: 5 min
Storage 14 days (minimum)

*This preserve has pretty much the same properties as those possessed by other preserves. A similar concoction can be made with an alternative main ingredient (such as carrots).*

1. Take a fresh long white radish. Scrape its outer skin, cut its top and bottom off and then cut it into large pieces. Using a fork, prick the pieces all over without breaking them.
2. Submerge the radish pieces in sufficient water in a microwave-compatible dish. Cover with kitchen paper and cook at full power for 5 minutes. Remove from the oven and drain off the water completely. Set the radish aside on a plate.
3. Pour the sugar syrup into the same cooking dish and heat, uncovered, at full power for 5 minutes, or until the syrup comes to a boil. Carefully add the radish pieces and continue to cook, at full power, for another 5 minutes, or until the syrup begins to thicken and the radish is well cooked but not disintegrating.
4. Remove from the heat and let it stand for 5 minutes before packing in a sterilized, airtight jar. To serve (usually cold), sprinkle with the rose water and decorate with a silver foil.

# Seib Ka Murabba

APPLE PRESERVE

*This enticing preserve is particularly appropriate for the student community. You can similarly make it using potatoes, instead.*

1. Wash the apples, slice off the tops and bottoms, then prick the whole apples all over, using a fork.
2. Place the apples in a large bowl. Mix the lime slake with sufficient water to cover the apples; soak them in the solution for 30 minutes. Rinse the fruit in several changes of cold water and dry them completely.
3. In a microwave-safe 1.8 litre/3 pint/7½ cup dish, heat the sugar syrup, uncovered, at full power for 5 minutes, or until the syrup comes to a boil. Remove from the oven and spoon off any scum from the surface.
4. Carefully drop the apples into the syrup, return the dish to the oven and continue cooking, uncovered, at full power for another 10 minutes, or until the syrup thickens and the apples are completely cooked.
5. Remove from the oven and leave to stand for 5 minutes. Pack in a sterilized, airtight jar. Serve each apple dribbled with a few drops of rose water and decorated with a foil.

Serves 4-8

450 g/1 lb firm apples
1 tablespoon lime slake
water, as necessary
600 ml/1 pint/2½ cups sugar
  syrup of 1-string strength
  (see p.39)
1 tablespoon rose water
gold foils, to serve

Prep 10 min
+ soaking time
Cooking 15 min
+ standing time 5 min
Storage 6 months (minimum)

# Mithaaiyaan

SWEETMEATS

*Indian sweets symbolize fun and festivity and are an institution in themselves. Domiciled in the third largest sugar producing country in the world, the Indians have an incredibly sweet tooth! There is a celebration of some sort almost every day of the year and there are special sweets to mark each occasion. Indians offer sweets to please the children and placate the gods; also, as a token of love, hospitality and to celebrate a happy occasion.*

*Most Indian sweets are milk-based and are out-standing food value. They are further strengthened by the addition of nuts and flavourings and thereby become rich and sustaining. The method of using milk the Indian way, however, is not that well known in the West, even though Indian sweets are gaining popularity here.*

*On offer in the following pages of this chapter are desserts like Lychee and Rice Pudding or Toast Royale; traditional sweets (sample, for instance, the Snazzy Coconut Globes, Almond Toffee or Regal Sweet Rice). Savour them cooked the modern microwave way and I am sure you will join the already burgeoning hordes of converts to Indian sweets.*

# Rabadee

## THICKENED MILK CREAM

Makes 150 ml/¼ pint/⅔ cup

600 ml/1 pint/2½ cups
  creamy whole milk
1 tablespoon sugar, or to
  taste
pinch of green cardamom
  powder
½ teaspoon rose water
silver foils, to garnish

Prep 5 min
Cooking 30 min
+ standing time 5 min

*This delectable concoction, usually served chilled, is offered as a dessert or a sweet snack. The finished preparation resembles a snazzy and fragrant double (or even treble) cream.*

1. Take a microwave-compatible casserole of 1.8 litre/3 pint/7½ cup capacity. Cook the milk, uncovered, at full power for 5 minutes.
2. Add the sugar and cardamom powder and blend thoroughly. Continue cooking for another 25 minutes, stirring every 5 or 6 minutes to break the skin forming on the top and encourage even thickening of the liquid.
3. When the milk has reduced to a quarter of the original quantity, or less if you prefer, the rabadee is ready. Remove from the oven and let it stand for 5 minutes. Refrigerate until ready to serve.
4. Sprinkle the rabadee with rose water and garnish each serving with a silver foil. Eat with a spoon.

# Chaawal Ki Kheer

RICE PUDDING

*The fragrant aroma of this best-known Indian pudding is hypnotic – it is nothing like the tinned variety sold in the supermarkets of the West! You can achieve your preferred thickness by adjusting the cooking times: cook longer for a thicker texture (a quicker method to achieve this would be to add double cream towards the end of the cooking time).*

1. Place the ghee and rice in an appropriate casserole of 1.8 litre/3 pint/7½ cup capacity. Microwave, uncovered, at full power for 2 minutes, stirring once.
2. Remove from the oven, add the sugar and milk and stir well. Cook, uncovered, at full power for 15 minutes, stirring 2 or 3 times in quick succession towards the end of the cooking time in order to break the skin forming on the surface.
3. Toss in the sultanas, pistachios and almonds and cook on high for another 3 minutes. Remove the casserole from the oven and let it stand for 5 minutes.
4. Sprinkle with the cardamom powder, before spooning into individual bowls, and decorate with foils.

Serves 4

2 teaspoons ghee
4 tablespoons basmati rice
100 g/4 oz/½ cup brown or white sugar, or to taste
600 ml/1 pint/2½ cups creamy whole milk
1 tablespoon sultanas or raisins, soaked
1 tablespoon flaked pistachios
1 tablespoon slivered almonds
½ teaspoon green cardamom powder
4 silver foils, to garnish

Prep 10 min
+ soaking time
Cooking 20 min
+ standing time 5 min

# Shaahi Tukray

## TOAST ROYALE

**Serves 4**

4 thick slices of bread
2 tablespoons ghee
150 ml/¼ pint/⅔ cup
   rabadee (see p.198)
1 tablespoon grated nuts,
such as almonds, cashews
   and pistachios
4 edible gold foils, to garnish
pinch of saffron stands, to
   garnish
kewra water, to serve

Prep 5 min
+ soaking time 5 min
Cooking 6 min

*This recipe transforms ordinary bread slices into a most stunning confection. Instead of rabadee, you can make it with 4 tablespoons each of 1-string sugar syrup (see p.39) and double cream and add a pinch of green cardamom powder. Usually served cold.*

1. Remove the crusts from the bread and cut each slice into 4 pieces.
2. Thickly smear the ghee on the surface of a large flat dish or plate and microwave on high for 1 minute. Arrange the bread pieces over the ghee and cook at full power for 3 minutes, turning over halfway through. Remove from the oven and arrange four pieces on each individual serving dish.
3. Heat the rabadee, uncovered, at full power for 2 minutes. Spoon it over the bread pieces and let the rabadee soak in for at least 5 minutes.
4. Sprinkle the nuts over the bread pieces and garnish each serving with a foil and a few strands of saffron. Squirt with a few drops of kewra water before serving.

# Leechi Ki Kheer

LYCHEE PUDDING

*Lychees are obtainable in season from Asian fruiterers and some supermarkets; alternatively, use the tinned variety but adjust the sugar content. The proof of this pudding is in its eating – it tastes out of this world!*

1. Place the milk in a bowl of 1.8 litre/3 pint/7½ cup capacity and microwave, uncovered, at full power for 10 minutes, stirring once or twice during cooking.

2. Add the lychee flesh and blend thoroughly, then stir in the sugar and nuts. Cook, uncovered, on high for another 8 minutes, stirring a couple of times towards the end of cooking to break the skin forming on the surface.

3. Remove from the oven and leave to stand for 5 minutes. Sprinkle the dessert with cardamom powder and garnish with the saffron strands. Serve hot or chilled, after dribbling some kewra water on each serving.

**Serves 4**

600 ml/1 pint/2½ cups
  creamy whole milk
100 g/4 oz/1 cup lychee flesh
100 g/4 oz/½ cup sugar, or to
  taste
50 g/2 oz/½ cup chopped
  nuts
½ teaspoon green
  cardamom powder
½ teaspoon saffron strands
kewra water, to serve

**Prep 10 min**
**Cooking 18 min**
**+ standing time 5 min**

# Shreekhand

## SAFFRON YOGHURT

**Serves 4**

450 g/1 lb/2½ cups plain
   yoghurt
175 g/6 oz/¾ cup sugar, or to
   taste
pinch of grated nutmeg
½ teaspoon green
   cardamom powder
1 tablespoon grated nuts,
   such as almonds,
   pistachios or walnuts
1 tablespoon rose water
pinch of saffron strands,
   crushed
fresh red rose petals,
   to decorate

**Prep 10 min**
**+ dripping time 2 hours**
**+ chilling 30 min**

*This delicious offering from the Maharashtra region of India is a particular favourite of people watching their weight. Eat it by itself, with a spoon, or with one of the Indian breads.*

1. Place the yoghurt in a clean muslin cloth, fold it up into a loose bundle and suspend it over a pan for about 2 hours or until all the excess moisture has dripped through. Discard the water.
2. Transfer the drained yoghurt from the muslin to a bowl. Add the sugar and whisk until the mixture is smooth. Stir in the nutmeg, cardamom, nuts and rose water and blend thoroughly.
3. Refrigerate for about 30 minutes. Sprinkle with the saffron and serve decorated with the rose petals.

# Naariyal Kheer Sugandh

SCENTED COCONUT PUDDING

*This superb pudding will, I am sure, be a hit with the whole family. The blend of coconut, dried fruits and rose water lends a distinctive flavour to the dish, and the taste is nothing short of ambrosial! Adjust the thickness of texture to your liking, with the concomitant regulation of cooking times.*

1. Place the ghee in a suitable 2.4 litre/4 pint/10 cup casserole and cook, covered, at full power for 1 minute. Stir in the coconut and continue cooking, covered, on high for another 2 minutes. Stir twice in between, to ensure even cooking of the coconut.

2. Add the milk and sugar and cook, uncovered, at full power for 12 minutes, stirring a couple of times to break the skin forming at the surface.

3. Stir in the dried fruits and nuts and the cardamom and cook, uncovered, at full power for a further 5 minutes, or until the milk is reduced by half.

4. Remove from the oven and stand for 5 minutes. Sprinkle with the saffron and splash a generous quantity of rose water on each serving.

Serves 4

50 g/2 oz/¼ cup ghee
100 g/4 oz/1 cup coconut
 (fresh or dried), grated
900 ml/1½ pints/3¾ cups
 creamy whole milk
75 g/3 oz sugar, or to taste
50 g/2 oz mixed dried fruits
 and nuts, such as sultanas,
 chironji nuts and slivered
 almonds
1 teaspoon green cardamom
 seeds
pinch of saffron strands
2 tablespoons rose water

Prep 10 min
Cooking 20 min
+ standing time 5 min

# Soutpheni Mewaa

FRUITY VERMICELLI CLUSTER

**Serves 4**

900 ml/1½ pints/3¾ cups
  creamy whole milk
100 g/4 oz/½ cup sugar, or to
  taste
50 g/2 oz soutpheni
2 tablespoons mixed slivered
  almonds and walnuts
½ teaspoon green
  cardamom powder
½ teaspoon saffron strands,
  crushed
silver foils, to garnish
1 tablespoon rose water,
  to serve

**Prep 5 min
+ chilling time
Cooking 10 min
+ standing time 5 min**

*This easy-to-cook dish is usually prepared to mark an occasion and contains soutpheni – ready-cooked discs of which are obtainable from good Asian grocers. Adjust the cooking times to accommodate the preferred thickness of milk. Another celebratory dish, called feerini, can be made the same way: substitute the soutpheni with 50 g/2 oz/½ cup rice flour, dissolved in 6 tablespoons of the measured milk. Add this mixture to the cooking milk at the same point as the soutpheni, but increase the cooking time by another 3 minutes.*

1. Combine the milk and sugar in a 2.4 litre/4 pint/10 cup microwave-compatible casserole and cook, uncovered, at full power for 8 minutes, or until the milk comes to a boil. Stir once or twice during cooking.
2. Remove from the oven, place the soutpheni discs over the milk and add the nuts and cardamom. Cook, uncovered, at full power for another 2 minutes. Let the mixture stand for 5 minutes before refrigerating for 30 minutes or more.
3. Sprinkle the saffron over the top of the dessert and decorate with silver foils before serving with a generous splash of rose water.

# Naariyal Laddu Shobha

## COCONUT GLOBES

*This is the darling dish which has attracted in droves converts to the world of Indian sweetmeats. A boon to those with a sweet tooth, this preparation is made very quickly indeed.*

1. In a deep microwave-safe bowl, place the khoya, half the sugar and half the coconut and microwave, uncovered, at full power for 5 minutes, stirring once or twice during cooking.
2. Add the remaining sugar and blend thoroughly. Cook, uncovered, on high for another 2 minutes.
3. Remove the mixture from the oven and let it stand for 5 minutes. Place the cardamom and remaining coconut on separate flat dishes.
4. When the mixture is sufficiently cool to handle, make about 16 small, walnut-sized balls from it. Roll these laddus over the coconut, sprinkle a little cardamom powder on each and serve hot or cold.

**Makes 16 globes (laddus)**

225 g/8 oz/1 cup khoya
  (see p.37)
175 g/6 oz/¾ cup sugar, or to
  taste
175g/6oz desiccated coconut
1 teaspoon green cardamom
  powder

**Prep 10 min**
**Cooking 7 min**
**+ standing time 5 min**

# Shaandaar Petha

## GOLDEN WHITEGOURD CUBES

**Makes 1 kg/35 oz**

450 g/1 lb whitegourd flesh
1 teaspoon edible lime slake
900 ml/1½ pints/3¾ cups
  sugar syrup at 1-string
  strength (see p.39)
edible gold foils, to garnish
2 tablespoons rose water, to
  serve

**Prep 15 min**
**+ soaking time**
**Cooking 15 min**
**+ standing time 5 min**

*This is a famous offering from Agra, the city of Taj Mahal. It can be served dry, or with syrup. To serve it dry, continue cooking the mixture until the sugar granulates – an additional 5 minutes or so. Serve hot or chilled.*

1. Cut the whitegourd into small cubes, prick them all over with a fork and place them in a large bowl. Make a solution by mixing the lime slake with enough water to cover the whitegourd cubes and pour it into the bowl. Leave to soak overnight. Next day, drain the cubes and rinse several times in cold running water.

2. Pour the syrup into a microwave-compatible casserole of 3.6 litre/6 pint/15 cup capacity and cook, uncovered, at full power for 5 minutes, or until the syrup comes to a boil. Stir once during heating. Remove from the oven and skim any scum from the surface.

3. Lower the cubes into the syrup and microwave at full power for 10 minutes, or until the gourd cubes are tender and golden, stirring occasionally. Make sure the syrup does not get too thick and that it has completely soaked into the cubes.

4. Remove from the oven and leave to stand for 5 minutes. Cover individual portions with the gold foils and serve with a sprinkling of rose water.

# Burfi Baadaam Khushbu

## PERFUMED ALMOND TOFFEE

*This burfi is good for encephalonic stimulation; ergo very popular with the intellectual community. The dish can also be made with coconut, cashew or pistachio nuts instead of ground almonds. Like other Indian sweetmeats, this dish is offered on happy, celebratory occasions.*

1. In a flat open dish, mix the ground almonds with sufficient milk to make a thick paste. Add 50g/2oz/¼ cup ghee and cook, uncovered, at full power for 2 minutes, stirring halfway through.
2. Add the khoya and mix thoroughly. Stir in another tablespoon of ghee and the desired amount of sugar syrup. Cook, uncovered, at full power for 5 minutes, stirring occasionally.
3. Remove the mixture from the oven, stir in the kewra water and leave to stand for 5 minutes.
4. Grease the base of a large platter with some more ghee and sprinkle the cardamom powder on its surface. Pour the cooked mixture over it, stirring, and, using a spatula, spread the mixture out evenly. Let it cool and set.
5. With a sharp knife, cut the mixture into squares or diamonds, turn them over and serve decorated with the gold foils.

Makes 675 g/1½ lb

450 g/1 lb ground almond
milk, as necessary
ghee, as necessary
225 g/8 oz/1 cup khoya
  (see p.37)
sugar syrup at 1-string
  strength (see p.39), to
  taste
kewra water, to taste
2 teaspoons green cardamom
  powder
edible gold foils, to decorate

Prep 15 min
Cooking 7 min
+ standing time 5 min

# Shaahi Zardaa (or Meethay Chaawal)
## REGAL SWEET RICE

**Serves 4**

1 tablespoon ghee
1 teaspoon green cardamom
  seeds
4 cloves
225 g/8 oz/1 cup basmati rice,
  soaked
150 ml/¼ pint/⅔ cup water
2 tablespoons sugar,
  or to taste
50 g/2 oz/½ cup mixed dried
  fruit and nuts such as
  almonds, cashews,
  pistachios and sultanas,
  chopped
pinch of saffron strands,
  crushed
edible gold foils, to serve

Prep 10 min
+ soaking time
Cooking 15 min
+ standing time 5 min

*The inclusion of nuts, saffron and gold foils makes this dish truly regal and colourful; the pastiche of flavours stands out like the smell of flowers on a landscape garden! This ambrosial delectation can be served on its own, or as the grand finale of a gorgeous meal.*

1. Place the ghee, cardamom seeds and cloves in a suitable casserole and cook, uncovered, at full power for 2 minutes or until the spices become aromatic.
2. Stir in the rice and cook, uncovered, at full power for another 3 minutes, stirring occasionally.
3. Stir in the water and half-cover the dish with the lid. Cook at full power for 5 minutes, or until the water is fully absorbed into the rice and the surface resembles a crumpet, with steaming holes all over the place!
4. Add the sugar and mixed fruit and nuts, stirring a few times. Reduce the heat setting to medium, cover and cook for another 5 minutes, or until the rice is tender and each grain is separate.
5. Remove the dish from the oven and sprinkle the saffron over the preparation. Leave, covered, to stand for 5 minutes then serve, garnished with gold foils.

# Kishmishee Gulgulay

MICROWAVE SULTANA FRITTERS

*Traditionally, gulgulay (plural of gulgulaa) are made for birthday parties. The ingredients used in India are jaggery and plain flour, and the mixture is deep-fried. I have adapted the concept to the microwave. These fritters are quick to make and taste great!*

1. Rub together the sugar and butter until the mixture is light and frothy. Stir in the flour and salt, then the egg and mix thoroughly. Stir in the sultanas and milk, then knead to give a smooth mixture.
2. Spoon the mixture into four small paper cups and arrange them in a circle on a plate. Cook, uncovered, at full power for 4 minutes, or until the fritters are done. If your microwave does not have a turntable, manually rotate the plate clockwise, a quarter turn per minute.
3. Remove the fritters from the oven and leave them to stand for 5 minutes. Serve hot.

Serves 4

2 tablespoons sugar, or to taste
25 g/1 oz butter
25 g/1 oz/¼ cup self-raising flour
tiny pinch of salt
1 large egg
25 g/1 oz sultanas, soaked
1 teaspoon milk

Prep 10 min
+ soaking time
Cooking 4 min
+ standing time 5 min

# Sujee Ka Halwa

GLISTENING SEMOLINA FUDGE

**Serves 4**

50 g/2 oz/¼ cup ghee
100 g/4 oz/⅔ cup fine
 semolina
150 ml/¼ pint/⅔ cup milk
100 g/4 oz/½ cup sugar, or to
 taste
50 g/2 oz/⅓ cup sultanas,
 soaked
25 g/1 oz/⅓ cup desiccated
 coconut
25 g/1 oz/¼ cup flaked
 almonds
1 teaspoon green cardamom
 powder
silver foils, to serve

**Prep 10 min
+ soaking time
Cooking 15 min
+ standing time 2 min**

*This 'dry' (moist, as opposed to curried) and fluffy preparation is a standard offering on many religious occasions in the Punjab. It is a light food for the breakfast table and very popular with all age groups. It can be refrigerated for a couple of weeks, or frozen for up to four months.*

1. Place the ghee and semolina in a microwave-compatible dish. Cook, covered, at full power for 3 minutes, stirring once.
2. Add the milk, sugar, sultanas, coconut, half the almonds and half the cardamom powder. Cook, uncovered, on high for 7 minutes, or until the mixture has blended and is boiling. Stir a couple of times during cooking.
3. Sprinkle the remaining almonds and cardamom over the preparation and continue to cook, uncovered, at full power for another 5 minutes. Remove the bowl from the oven and leave to stand for 2 minutes. Stir, then serve hot or cold, garnishing each serving with a silver foil.

# Gaajar Ka Shaandaar Halwa

GLOSSY CARROT FUDGE

*This offering from Northern India is normally eaten by itself but it can also be served, topped with cream, as a dessert. It is served hot or cold and can be reheated a second or third time without losing its flavour. Store any leftovers in a covered container in the refrigerator – they will last for several days.*

1. Wash, scrape and grate the carrots into long, fine strips. Place the ghee and carrots in a microwave-safe deep dish. Cover and cook on high for 2 minutes, stirring halfway through cooking.
2. Stir in the milk and khoya and cook, uncovered, at full power for 13 minutes, or until the milk is fully absorbed into the carrots and has blended with the khoya. Stir a couple of times during the cooking period.
3. Add the sugar then stir in the almonds, pistachios and cardamom. Blend thoroughly and cook, uncovered, at full power for another 5 minutes.
4. Remove the halwa from the oven and leave to stand for 5 minutes. Stir a few times then add the saffron and kewra water. Garnish with the foil, and you are ready to serve.

**Serves 4**

450 g/1 lb tender carrots
100 g/4 oz/½ cup ghee
300 ml/½ pint/1¼ cups creamy whole milk
175 g/6 oz/1 cup granulated khoya (see p.37)
175 g/6 oz/¾ cup sugar, or to taste
1 tablespoon slivered almonds
1 tablespoon chopped pistachio nuts
pinch of coarsely ground green cardamom seeds
pinch of saffron strands
1 tablespoon kewra water
edible gold foils, to garnish

**Prep 15 min**
**Cooking 20 min**
**+ standing time 5 min**

# Peya aur Kulfiyaan

## BEVERAGES AND ICE CREAM

*Hot and cold soft drinks and ice creams occupy a pride of place in the Indian cookery calendar. India seems to have an inexhaustible store of all of these. It has to be said that not all these dishes need cooking, and some require cooking only in part. The microwave takes care of what cooking is required beautifully. The net result in each case is a stunning offering. All these dishes lend themselves to endless possibilities in terms of variation and experimentation.*

*Hot drinks are essential for those who live in cold countries, and others too. Tea is the main offering of the Indian repertoire of hot drinks and a large variety of tea preparations is made in the country. It is said that tea warms you up in winter and cools you down in summer. Tea has become the symbol of civilization in the world today, and India exports mega-tons of that civilization to the West!*

*Coffee is grown in large quantities in several parts of India. It is the staple drink of the whole of south India. Coffee-drinking denotes sophistication and modernity. Coffee houses are dotted all over India, especially around the universities and other haunts of the intelligentsia.*

*It is fashionable in India for the hostess to serve her guests with a freshly made lassi or sharbat. At the end of a scorching day, these cool drinks in long glasses appear more seductive than anything on two legs! A tip for garnish: most of these drinks are served with ice. May I suggest you make larger quantities and freeze part of the drink in ice cube trays, so as to have at least two ice cubes per serving. Your guests are bound to be impressed by your presentation skills when you offer them drinks with colour-coded ice cubes!*

*The scrumptious Indian ice creams are still not widely known in the West, although they do make an occasional appearance here and there. They are rich dishes (no joy here for the weight-watching faint-hearts!), of harder consistency than normal ice creams. In the absence of a preservative, like gelatine, these ice creams melt very quickly, so don't leave theme in the open for long; serve straight from the freezer, or via the refrigerator.*

*The traditional way of making kulfi is to cook the milk preparation, pour it into long conical tin moulds with tightly fitting lids, and to freeze it in earthen pitchers. I suggest a modern alternative: use ice cube trays or other similar containers as moulds, and stick them in the freezer for an hour or longer. All the kulfi dishes can be served with faaluda and therefore faaluda has not always been mentioned in individual recipes.*

# Nawaabi Chaay

PRINCELY TEA

*This tea is traditionally reserved for the upper echelons of Indian society. Given that it is so easy to make in the microwave – and most households possess a microwave – this beverage could soon emerge as the hot favourite of the bosses and workers alike!*

1. Place the water, milk and cardamom pods in a microwave-proof measuring jug of 1.2 litre/2 pint/5 cup capacity.
Heat, uncovered, at full power for 5 minutes.
2. Add the tea and sugar and continue to cook, uncovered, for 1 more minute.
3. Remove the jug from the oven. Add the saffron, cover and leave to stand for 1 minute. Serve steaming hot in demitasse cups.

Serves 4

300 ml/½ pint/1¼ cups
  water
300 ml/½ pint/1¼ cups
  creamy whole milk
2 green cardamom pods
2 tablespoons tea leaves, or 4
  tea bags
sugar, to taste
pinch of saffron strands

Prep 2 min
Cooking 6 min
+ standing time 1 min

# Masaali Chaay

SPICED TEA

Serves 4

600 ml/1 pint/2½ cups water
2 cloves
1 brown cardamom, cracked
4 black peppercorns
2.5cm/1 inch cinnamon stick,
  broken
4 basil leaves
2 teaspoons Darjeeling or
  Assam tea, or 4 tea bags
300 ml/½ pint/1¼ cups
  milk
4 teaspoons sugar, or to taste

Prep 2 min
Cooking 7 min
+ standing time 2 min

*One step ahead of herbal tea, the only herb in this brew is basil (tulsi); the rest are spices. This tea is invigorating and refreshes the parts the other teas cannot reach. It is also taken as a cure for the common cold and can be made in a jiffy in the microwave. Serve hot or cold (chilled and/or with ice).*

1. Place the water in a microwave-friendly measuring jug of around 1.8 litre/3 pint/7½ cup capacity. Heat, uncovered, at full power for 5 minutes, or until the water comes to a boil.
2. Add the cloves, cardamom, peppercorns, cinnamon, basil and tea and continue to cook, uncovered, at full power for another 2 minutes.
3. Remove from the oven. Add the milk and sugar, cover, and leave to stand for 2 minutes. Stir and strain before serving.

# Adrak Ki Meethi Chaay

SWEET GINGER TEA

*Ginger has digestive properties and provides inner warmth. This particular preparation is regarded as a panacea for colds, coughs and runny nose. Serve hot any time of the day or night.*

1. Place the crushed ginger and the measured water in a microwave-safe casserole. Cook, half-covered, at full power for 4 minutes, or until the water comes to a boil.
2. Add the sugar and milk. Continue to cook, covered, at full power for another 2 minutes. Remove the tea from the oven and stir and strain it. Serve very hot.

Serves 4

2.5 cm/1 inch piece root
    ginger, crushed
600 ml/1 pint/2½ cups water
4 teaspoons sugar, or to taste
300 ml/½ pint/1¼ cups milk

Prep 5 min
Cooking 6 min

# Vaadi-e-Kashmir Chaay

TEA FROM HEAVEN-ON-EARTH

**Serves 4**

2 teaspoons green tea leaves
900 ml/1½ pints/3¾ cups
  creamy whole milk
2 tablespoons sugar, or to
  taste
4 green cardamom pods,
  cracked
2.5 cm/1 inch cinnamon stick,
  broken
1 tablespoon chopped
  almonds

**Prep 2 min**
**Cooking 8 min**
**+ standing time 1 min**

*The residents regard Kashmir as heaven on earth and they are very proud of their rich and spicy tea. The crocus farmers (producing the most expensive spice – saffron), and other workers carry ready-made hot tea on their person, which keeps them warm and supplies them with a drink.*

1. Place all the ingredients in a suitable measuring jug or casserole of 1.8 litre/3 pint/7½ cup capacity and cook, half-covered, at full power for 8 minutes, or until boiling. Stir halfway through cooking.
2. Remove the container from the oven, stir and leave to stand, tightly covered, for 1 minute. Stir and strain the tea before serving.

# Kaafi Malaai

CREAMED COFFEE

*This fabulous beverage brings the West that much closer to the East! Feel free to experiment with your own alternative methods of cooking, or topping.*

1. In a microwave-friendly covered dish of 1.2 litre/2 pint/5 cup capacity, make a paste with the coffee granules and a little water. Add the rest of the measured water and cook, half-covered, on high for 8 minutes.
2. Stir in the cardamom and sugar and continue to cook at full power for 2 minutes.
3. Remove the dish from the oven, cover it tightly and leave to stand for 2 minutes. Then stir and serve the coffee piping hot, topped with cream.

Serves 4

2 tablespoons coffee
  granules
600 ml/1 pint/2½ cups water
pinch of green cardamom
  powder
2 tablespoons sugar, or to
  taste
4 tablespoons/⅓ cup
  whisked double cream

Prep 5 min
Cooking 10 min
+ standing time 2 min

# Meethi Preeti Lassi

## SATSUMA-HONEY LOVE AFFAIR

Serves 4

300 ml/½ pint/1¼ cups
   plain yoghurt
300 ml/½ pint/1¼ cups icy
   cold water
300 ml/½ pint/1¼ cups fresh
   orange juice
1 tablespoon honey
1 tablespoon sugar
4 tablespoons crushed ice
1 teaspoon rose water
2 tablespoons slivered
   almonds
orange slices, to garnish

Prep 10 min

*This lovely drink is made in a jiffy. Many variations are possible. Adjust the amount of water to obtain the desired consistency, and sugar, to obtain the level of sweetness you like.*

1. Mix the yoghurt, water and orange juice and whisk thoroughly. Stir in the honey, sugar and ice, and whisk again.
2. Sprinkle the rose water over the liquid. Top each serving with almonds and garnish with orange slices.

# Peeyush Barsaat

RAIN OF NECTAR

*This drink is often made on religious occasions and served in small quantities as prasaad (gift from the gods). It is also known as panchaamrit (five nectars). It is usually thick in consistency and not, by tradition, chilled. However, feel free to vary on both counts.*

1. Place the milk and yoghurt in a deep bowl and whisk together. Stir in the sugar and mix until it dissolves.
2. Add the honey and then the dried fruits and nuts. Stir thoroughly and serve, sprinkled with the rose water.

Serves 4

600 ml/1 pint/2½ cups whole creamy milk

300 ml/½ pint/1¼ cups plain yoghurt

2 tablespoons sugar, or to taste

25 g/1 oz/4 tablespoons honey

100 g/4 oz/1 cup mixed dried fruits and nuts, such as chopped coconut, lotus puffs, chironji nuts and sultanas/raisins

rose water, to serve

Prep 10 min

# Gulabi Manoj Tarbooz Tarang

ROSY WATERMELON PUNCH

**Serves 4**

225 g/8 oz/2 cups ripe,
  seedless watermelon flesh
4 tablespoons/⅓ cup sugar
600 ml/1 pint/2½ cups ice
  cold water
½ teaspoon green
  cardamom powder
8 ice cubes, crushed
1 teaspoon rose water
1 tablespoon fresh rose
  petals

**Prep 10 min**

*When watermelons are in season, the making of this punch is truly a pleasure. Another lightweight and refreshing drink with several possible variations.*

1. Place the melon flesh in a clean cloth and extract the juice by squeezing it tightly, or liquidize the watermelon in a juicer, blender or food processor.
2. Add the sugar, water, cardamom and ice and whisk thoroughly. Serve sprinkled with rose water and topped with rose petals.

# Pawan Anaar Baarish

POMEGRANATE SHOWER

*This soft drink is very rejuvenating and restores composure after a hard day's work. It is especially enjoyable in the rainy season (which is almost every second day in Britain!), when the raindrops are falling and there is a gentle breeze. You can either buy bottled pomegranate juice or make it fresh yourself: crush the seeds of the fruit to squeeze out the juice.*

1. Place the sugar and water in a deep vessel and whisk until the sugar has completely dissolved.
2. Stir in the pomegranate juice, food colouring and rose water and mix thoroughly. Chill for 30 minutes and serve garnished with lemon slices.

**Serves 4**

4 tablespoons/⅓ cup sugar
600 ml/1 pint/2½ cups water
300 ml/½ pint/1¼ cups
   pomegranate juice
4 drops red food colouring
1 tablespoon rose water
lemon slices, to garnish

**Prep 10 min
+ chilling time**

# Mohit Neebu Sharbat

LEMON SHERBET

**Serves 4**

600 ml/1 pint/2¹/₂ cups water
1 tablespoon lemon juice
2 tablespoons sugar
1 teaspoon kewra water
8 ice cubes, crushed
lemon slices, to garnish

**Prep 5 min**

*This soft drink is one of the most popular; athletes are particularly partial to it because no other drink is as refreshing after strenuous activity. The quantities of lemon juice and sugar should be adapted to personal taste.*

1. Mix the water, lemon juice, sugar and kewra water, together with half the ice, and whisk briskly.
2. Serve the drink, topped with the remaining crushed ice and garnished with lemon slices.

# Roshan Faaluda

## COOL VERMICELLI

*Faaluda is the inevitable companion of Indian ice creams (kulfiyaan). It is a collective name given to jelly-like translucent bright strands made out of cornflour or arrowroot. It can be served by itself too, in which case sprinkle it with sugar syrup (see p.39), crushed ice and some kewra water.*

**Serves 6**

600 ml/1 pint/2½ cups water
175 g/6 oz/1½ cups cornflour

**Prep 5 min**
**Cooking 12 min**
**+ standing time 5 min**

1. Using a little of the water, make a paste from the cornflour and whisk until there are no lumps. Gradually mix in the rest of the measured water to make a batter.
2. Place the batter in a microwave-compatible covered dish of 1.8 litre/3 pint/7½ cup capacity. Microwave, uncovered, at full power for 8 minutes, or until the batter comes to a boil.
3. Stir then cover and continue to cook at full power for another 4 minutes, or until the mixture becomes thick and translucent. Remove the casserole from the oven and leave to stand, covered, for 5 minutes.
4. Half-fill a large ordinary saucepan with cold water. Place a jhanna (a metal stirrer with a large handle and a perforated disc at the end) across the mouth of the saucepan. Rub the cornflour mixture over the jhanna so that large vermicelli-like strands (faaluda) will begin to drop into the saucepan. When all the flour mixture is used up and the faaluda is made, change the water in the pan a few times, taking care the strands are not broken.
5. Leave the faaluda to stand in clear cold water. Serve 1 tablespoon (or more) of the strands straight from the pan with each serving of kulfi. Leftover faaluda can go into the refrigerator, placed in water in a covered container.

# Pishtay Ki Kulfi

PISTACHIO ICE CREAM

**Serves 4**

225 g/8 oz/1 cup pistachios
300 ml/½ pint/1¼ cups
  creamy whole milk
300 ml/½ pint/1¼ cups
  single cream
2 tablespoons sugar
pinch of salt
½ teaspoon kewra water

**Prep 10 min**
**+ freezing time**
**Cooking 13 min**
**+ standing time 5 min**

*This kulfi is truly delicious. If it proves too expensive, use only half the prescribed quantity of pistachio and make up the difference with green food colouring in water, plus some pistachio essence.*

1. Finely grind the pistachios with a little of the milk. Place the paste in a microwave-safe casserole of 1.8 litre/3 pint/7½ cup capacity and add the rest of the milk. Cook, uncovered, at full power for 8 minutes, or until the milk comes to a boil. Stir once or twice during cooking to break the skin that forms on the surface.
2. Add the cream, sugar and salt and stir thoroughly. Continue cooking, covered, at full power for another 5 minutes, stirring once.
3. Remove from the oven and let the casserole stand, without cover, for 5 minutes, to cool.
4. When cool, fill the mixture into moulds and freeze. Serve straight from the freezer, if serving with the whole meal at the outset, or after a brief transfer into the refrigerator, if serving for immediate consumption. Sprinkle each serving with kewra water.

# Phalon Ki Kulfi

## TUTTI FRUTTI

*Try to obtain and use fresh and genuine fruits for this dish, but feel free to substitute fruits of your choice. The milk mixture for this kulfi should be thick and creamy. Its taste will then take you to the seventh heaven!*

1. Place the milk in a microwave-proof covered casserole of 1.2 litre/2 pint/5 cup capacity. Cook, uncovered, at full power for 8 minutes, or until the milk comes to a boil. Stir once during cooking to break the skin forming on the surface.
2. Stir in the cream, fruits, sugar and salt. Cover and continue to cook at full power for another 6 minutes, stirring halfway through.
3. Remove the mixture from the oven and leave it to stand, without cover, for 5 minutes, to cool. Use this mixture to fill containers of your choice and freeze. Sprinkle with kewra water before serving.

**Serves 4**

300 ml/½ pint/1¼ cups
  creamy whole milk
6 tablespoons/½ cup double
  cream
4 tablespoons chopped fruit,
  such as mango, lychee,
  cape gooseberry
2 tablespoons sugar
pinch of salt
kewra water, to serve

**Prep 10 min
+ freezing time
Cooking 14 min
+ standing time 5 min**

# Mewaa Malaai Kulfi

NUTTY ICE CREAM

Serves 4

pinch of saffron strands,
   crushed
1 teaspoon rose water
600ml/1 pint/2½ cups
   creamy whole milk
½ teaspoon green
   cardamom powder
1 tablespoon slivered
   almonds, crushed
1 tablespoon desiccated
   coconut
1 tablespoon chironji nuts,
   chopped
2 tablespoons sugar
pinch of salt

Prep 5 min
+ freezing time
Cooking 15 min
+ standing time 5 min

*Whether you are a prince or a pauper, this simply-made kulfi will surely leave you ecstatic. Faaluda (see p.225) will make it more visually attractive.*

1. In a small bowl, leave the saffron to steep in the rose water for 5 or so minutes.
2. Place the milk in a microwave-safe covered casserole of 1.8 litre/3 pint/7½ cup capacity and heat, uncovered, at full power for 15 minutes, or until the volume of milk is reduced roughly by half. Stir every 5 minutes to break the skin forming on the surface.
3. Remove the milk from the oven and add the mixture of saffron and rose water plus all the remaining ingredients. Stir well then tightly cover with the lid and leave to stand for 5 minutes.
4. Fill the mixture into moulds and freeze. Serve from the freezer, or via the refrigerator.

# Phaalsa-Khubaani Kulfi

BLACKCURRANT AND PEACHES

*This is another rich fruit ice cream, but one made in a different way. A very pleasant and delectable kulfi indeed. Do serve it with faaluda (see p.225).*

1. Place the water in a microwave-proof casserole of 1.2 litre/2 pint/5 cup capacity. Cook, covered, at full power for 6 minutes, or until the water comes to a boil.
2. Remove the casserole from the oven. Lift the lid and drop the fruits into the boiling water. Leave to stand, uncovered, for 5 minutes. When the water cools, remove the fruits and skin them. Then purée them in a blender or food processor.
3. Add the puréed fruit mixture to the milk and cream, blending well. Pour into containers and freeze. Serve straight from the freezer, or via the refrigerator, after sprinkling with kewra water.

Serves 4

600 ml/1 pint/2½ cups water
8 juicy blackcurrants
4 large peaches
150 ml/¼ pint/⅔ cup condensed milk
6 tablespoons/½ cup double cream
kewra water, to serve

Prep 5 min
+ freezing time
Cooking 6 min
+ standing time 5 min

# Kishan Kulfi

### CARDAMOM ICE CREAM

**Serves 4**

600 ml/1 pint/2½ cups
  creamy whole milk
100 g/4 oz/1 cup khoya
  (see p.37)
2 tablespoons sugar
1 teaspoon green cardamom
  powder
1 tablespoon grated
  pistachios
1 tablespoon rose water, to
  serve

Prep 5 min
+ freezing time
Cooking 12 min
+ standing time 5 min

*It is said that Lord Krishna (Kishan) was partial to this scrumptious kulfi. Be that as it may, there is no doubt that this luscious recipe tastes heavenly.*

1. Place the milk in a microwave-friendly casserole of 1.8 litre/3 pint/7½ cup capacity. Heat, uncovered, at full power for 8 minutes, stirring occasionally to break the skin forming on the surface.
2. Gradually add the khoya and stir. Then add the sugar, cardamom and pistachios. Cover and cook at full power for 4 minutes, stirring halfway through.
3. Remove the casserole from the oven and let it stand, uncovered, for 5 minutes. When cool, pour the mixture into moulds. Leave the moulds in the freezer for at least 1 hour, by which time the kulfi will be solid. Serve straight from the freezer, or via the refrigerator, sprinkled with rose water.

# Meera Kela Kulfi

BANANA ICE CREAM

*Meera Baai, although a member of royalty, was a great devotee of Lord Krishna. Most of her time was spent on worship and she lived on concoctions made from milk and fruits, like this one. You will go crackers after tasting it.*

1. Place the milk in a microwave-compatible covered dish of 1.8 litre/3 pint/7½ cup capacity. Cook, uncovered, on high for 5 minutes, stirring once towards the end.
2. Add the cream, banana, sugar and salt to the milk. Stir, cover and continue to cook at full power for another 5 minutes.
3. Remove the dish from the oven. Uncover and sprinkle with the cardamom powder. Leave to stand, uncovered, for 5 minutes.
4. When cool, pour the mixture into moulds and freeze. When ready to eat, take the kulfi out of the container (after it has travelled from the freezer, via refrigerator on to a plate), and cut it into round slices. Serve with a generous sprinkling of kewra water, and add 1 tablespoon of faaluda (see p.225) to each serving.

Serves 4

300 ml/½ pint/1¼ cups creamy whole milk
6 tablespoons/½ cup double cream
1 ripe banana, peeled and chopped
2 tablespoons sugar
pinch of salt
1 teaspoon green cardamom powder
1 tablespoon kewra water, to serve

Prep 5 min
+ freezing time
Cooking 10 min
+ standing time 5 min